NATIONAL GEOGRAPHIC DIRECTIONS

ALSO BY ANNA QUINDLEN

IMAGINED LONDON

IMAGINED LONDON

*A Tour of the World's
Greatest Fictional City*

ANNA QUINDLEN

NATIONAL GEOGRAPHIC DIRECTIONS

NATIONAL GEOGRAPHIC
Washington, D.C.

Published by the National Geographic Society
1145 17th Street, N.W., Washington, D.C. 20036-4688

Text copyright © 2004 Anna Quindlen
Map copyright © 2004 National Geographic Society

First printing September, 2004
Paperback edition 2006, ISBN 0-7922-4207-6

Photography Credits: PAGES 30, 34, 46, 102, 113–Lawrence Porges; PAGES 10, 50, 68–Bettmann/ CORBIS; PAGES 13, 119–Hulton-Deutsch Collection/CORBIS; PAGES 93, 146–CORBIS; PAGES 122, 155–Sophie Bassouls/CORBIS; PAGE 158–Julien Hekimian/Corbis Sygma

Library of Congress Cataloging-in-Publication Data
Quindlen, Anna
    Imagined London: a tour of the world's greatest fictional city / Anna Quindlen.
        p. cm. -- (National Geographic directions)
    ISBN: 0-7922-6561-0
        1. Literary landmarks--England--London. 2. English literature--England--London--History and criticism. 3. Authors, English--Homes and haunts--England--London. 4. London (England)--Description and travel. 5. London (England)--In literature. I. Title. II. Series

    PR110.L6Q35 2004
    820.9'9421--dc22

                                                            2004049958

One of the world's largest nonprofit scientific and educational organizations, the National Geographic Society was founded in 1888 "for the increase and diffusion of geographic knowledge." Fulfilling this mission, the Society educates and inspires millions every day through its magazines, books, television programs, videos, maps and atlases, research grants, the National Geographic Bee, teacher workshops, and innovative classroom materials. The Society is supported through membership dues, charitable gifts, and income from the sale of its educational products. This support is vital to National Geographic's mission to increase global understanding and promote conservation of our planet through exploration, research, and education.

For more information, please call 1-800-NGS LINE (647-5463), write to the Society at the above address, or visit the Society's Web site at www.nationalgeographic.com.

Interior design by Melissa Farris

Printed in the U.S.A.

For Amanda Urban, in lieu—
at least for now—of a mews house

IMAGINED LONDON

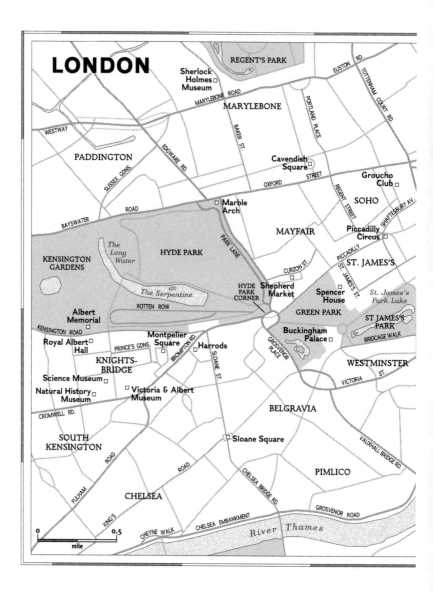

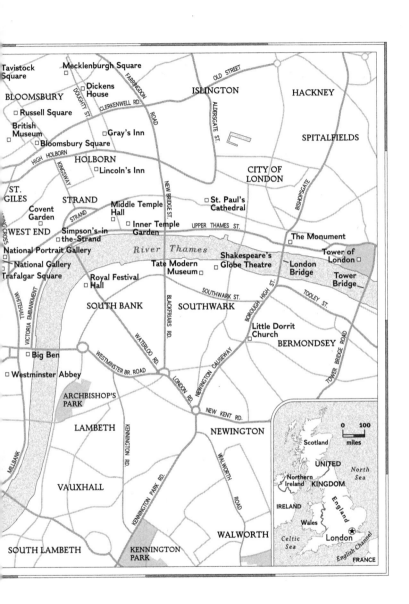

Tavistock Square

Mecklenburgh Square

Dickens House

FARRINGDON ROAD

OLD STREET

ISLINGTON

HACKNEY

BLOOMSBURY

DOUGHTY ST

CLERKENWELL RD.

ALDERSGATE ST.

Russell Square

British Museum

Gray's Inn

Bloomsbury Square

SPITALFIELDS

HIGH HOLBORN

HOLBORN

KINGSWAY

Lincoln's Inn

CITY OF LONDON

ST. GILES

STRAND

NEW BRIDGE ST.

St. Paul's Cathedral

BISHOPSGATE

Covent Garden

STRAND

Middle Temple Hall

WEST END

Inner Temple Garden

UPPER THAMES ST.

Simpson's-in-the-Strand

KING CROSS

National Portrait Gallery

National Gallery

Trafalgar Square

River Thames

Tate Modern Museum

Shakespeare's Globe Theatre

The Monument

London Bridge

Tower of London

Royal Festival Hall

BLACKFRIARS RD.

SOUTH BANK

SOUTHWARK

SOUTHWARK ST.

BOROUGH HIGH ST.

TOOLEY ST.

Tower Bridge

WHITEHALL

VICTORIA EMBANKMENT

Little Dorrit Church

BERMONDSEY

TOWER BRIDGE ROAD

Big Ben

WATERLOO RD.

Westminster Abbey

WESTMINSTER BR. ROAD

LONDON RD.

NEWINGTON CAUSEWAY

MILLBANK

ARCHBISHOP'S PARK

KENNINGTON RD.

NEW KENT RD.

LAMBETH

NEWINGTON

WALWORTH ROAD

KENNINGTON PARK RD.

VAUXHALL

SOUTH LAMBETH

KENNINGTON PARK

WALWORTH

0   100
miles

Scotland

UNITED

North Sea

Northern Ireland   KINGDOM

England

IRELAND

Wales

Celtic Sea

London

English Channel

FRANCE

CHAPTER ONE

On a rather mild early spring morning in 1995, a taxi pulled up to one of the low flat-faced old buildings that make up most of the block of Dean Street just north of Shaftesbury Avenue in London. The driver was perturbed. From the moment he had pulled out of the terminal at Heathrow Airport, he had tried to convince his passenger that no woman would want to be dropped off, suitcase in hand, at the address she had given at 8 a.m. on a Sunday. As he unloaded her luggage from what she called his trunk and he called his boot, he squinted with unconcealed hostility at the front of the house and the small sign that identified it as the Groucho

Club, so named because the writers and journalists and other non-clubby types who'd founded it liked the idea, expressed in the words of Groucho Marx, of never belonging to a place that would have them as a member.

There was no one on the street, and no one immediately visible behind the desk in the club, for that matter. The neighborhood was a nighttime neighborhood, a neighborhood of long dinners out and shutting down the pubs and streets crowded at midnight, so that sometimes you had to step off the curb to go on your way. And it had the sad and tired and slightly disreputable look that all such neighborhoods have on a Sunday morning, that look of the morning after the night before, the look of a full ashtray or a wineglass with dregs and a ring of blood red around the bottom, the look that a dress removed in haste after a party has on the floor of your bedroom in the bright sunlight. It had the look of a place in which everyone slept on Sundays until at least noon.

"Soho," the driver had said, and there was the sound of a curled lip in his broad British tones. He might as well have said "Sodom."

"A mistake's been made," he added before he slammed shut the hatch to his trunk, or boot, and drove off on the lookout for more sensible passengers.

But there was no mistake. An attendant who appeared to be slightly hungover, or at least very tired, produced a room key from behind the desk of the club. The small lobby outside the bar smelled strongly of cigarette smoke, and there was no lift. No lift, she thought to herself, and her heart thumped, not at the notion of hauling heavy suitcases up narrow stairs, which turned out to be a pain by the second landing, but because she had managed to use the word lift without thinking twice about it. Lift. Loo. Treacle. Trifle. As she thump-thumped up the stairs, like Christopher Robin dragging Pooh by the leg, only much more arduously, she silently practiced her English. Trainers. Waistcoats. Salad rolls.

The room was extremely small, exactly the sort of snug and vaguely uncomfortable place in which people who do not write imagine writers writing. If she had tried to write there, it would have had to be on the bed, which took up most of the available space. There was a bathroom shoehorned into one corner of the room—or was it more properly called a loo? Or just the bath, in the fashion of the Mitford sisters?—with a toilet in which, she could not help feeling every time she looked at it, shamefaced at being so obviously American, there was far too little water. The electrical sockets looked highly unfamiliar, and again there was that thump from within. She had purchased an adapter! She could convert the current!

She went to the window and looked out on a vast array of chimney pots and a sky the color of ash that came down so low that it seemed to have been responsible for the way in which so many of the chimney pots were leaning. She unpacked quickly and went downstairs, peeking into the door of the bar. No one was serving breakfast. There was garbage nestled around the curb outside. She walked for three blocks, found a newsstand, bought the *Sunday Times,* the *Independent on Sunday,* the *Observer,* and the *News of the World,* and somehow managed to stumble upon the timbered Tudor front of Liberty of London, the estimable department store. The scarf slung around her shoulders had come from Liberty by way of an intermediary shop on Madison Avenue.

The cafés she passed by seemed to promise coffee later. A few had people inside, filling pastry cases and setting out cups in the half-gloom of a business on the verge of opening. She lost track of where she was going and wound up on a street filled with peep shows and shops that sold sex toys and ridiculous lingerie, slashed panties, leopard print corsets. She doubled back on herself and was clearly in Chinatown, like every Chinatown on Earth, phony street pagodas and gilt-and-scarlet lanterns and restaurant names that sounded as if they'd been ineptly translated. Somehow she wound up on

Shaftesbury again, and suddenly, around one corner, she was face-to-face with a tiny dollhouse of a place in the Tudor style at the center of a deserted square. She thought it looked like a place where Henry VIII would have kept his hunting dogs. A block on and she found herself on Charing Cross Road, then in an enormous cobblestoned piazza. A small café was open on the corner, and she sat at a table and spread out her newspapers.

"I'm lost," she said to the young woman who wiped the table down.

"I wouldn't think so," she drawled, pointing out the window. "That's Covent Garden."

"Covent Garden," she thought to herself. "I'm in Covent Garden." And she felt full and foolish, both at the same time.

CHAPTER TWO

This is the story of a woman and the city she loved before she'd ever been there. The city, of course, is London, and the woman is me. Before I was a novelist, or a journalist, or even an adult, I felt about London the way most children my age felt about pen pals. I knew it well, but only at a distance, and only through words. Since the age of five I had been one of those people who was an indefatigable reader, more inclined to go off by myself with a book than do any of the dozens of things that children usually do to amuse themselves. I never aged out of it.

I was not an athlete or, in the vernacular of the English novels I devoured, was not good at games. I read and reread and recommended and rarely rejected, became one of those readers who will read trashy stories as long as they're not too terrible—well, even perhaps the truly terrible ones—and will reread something she's already read, even if it's something like a detective novel, when you'd suspect that knowing who had really killed the countess would materially detract from the experience. (It doesn't, and besides, I often can't remember who the murderer was in the first place.) I've remained that sort of reader to the present day, when my work as a novelist and an essayist means there is a lot more premium in it from a professional point of view. Aside from New York City, where I grew up as a person and as a reporter, the places where I most feel at home are bookstores and libraries.

And London.

The first time I recall visiting the great metropolis, I was sitting in a chair in a suburb of Philadelphia. The city streets were filled with fog and the cobbled pavers were slightly slick with moisture, so that the man and woman struggling down the street beneath the yellowed lamps slid on the street's surface. It was just after the war, and some of the buildings were empty holes left over from the bombs of the blitz. The book describing all this was by Patricia Wentworth, one of the series of mystery novels she wrote that often took place in country shires but wound up always, inevitably, in the capital, at the cozy flat of what I believed at the time to be the essential English spinster, a former governess named Maud Silver.

I have since been to London too many times to count in the pages of books, to Dickensian London rich with narrow alleyways and jocular street scoundrels, to the London of Conan Doyle and Margery Allingham with its salt-of-the-Earth police officers, troubled aristocrats, and crowded train stations. Hyde Park, Green Park, Soho, and Kensington: I had been to them all in my imagination before I ever set foot in England. So that by the time I actually visited London in 1995 for the first time, it felt less like an introduction and more like a homecoming. Here, I thought, is where Evelyn Waugh's bright young things danced until dawn, where Agatha Runcible, Lady Metroland's daughter, and the Honourable Miles Malpractice played. Here is where David Copperfield sought his fortune, and where Adam Dalgliesh has his spare and private flat.

The portraits of New York in literature are undoubtedly vivid ones, from the gentry of Edith Wharton peering from carriages on Fifth Avenue to the nouveau riche of Tom Wolfe reflexively painting their dining rooms red. Paris is well served by Hugo, and the coal mines of Wales are a living thing in D. H. Lawrence's *Sons and*

Evelyn Waugh in the 1930s

Lovers. Yet London has always been the star of literature, both because of the primacy of English literature in the canon and the rich specificity of the descriptions of the city contained in everything from Ngaio Marsh's mystery stories to Elizabeth Jane Howard's *Cazelet Chronicle.* A student of literature could walk through London and move within blocks from the great books of the eighteenth century to the detective stories of the twentieth to the new modernist tradition of the twenty-first.

For those of us who are overwrought readers, what that comes to mean is that there is really only one capital city in the world. Oh, there are the Russian towns of Chekhov and the St. Petersburg of Tolstoy and the Germany of Thomas Mann. I remember reading an undistinguished novel that affected me a great deal as a teenager about a young woman living in Krakow, which I had never heard of until then, and, of course, there was the Amsterdam of the Frank family, but diminished to an impossible cipher in the shadow of the attic setting that set the entire tone for *The Diary of a Young Girl.*

And for an American child, there are certainly many stories set in America. But they are stories ranging all over the great sprawling subcontinent, from Willa Cather's *My Antonia* in the Midwest to Steinbeck's *East of Eden* in California to the Massachusetts Bay Colony of *The Scarlet Letter.* American literature ranges north to south, east to west; it is not concentrated in one place, one place that becomes alive in books as though it is a hologram taking clear three-dimensional shape just past the open covers and the turned pages.

For an inveterate reader, there is only one city that comes utterly alive in mind in that fashion. Henry James, an American whose novels became exemplars of his contempt for his own country and its people and his sometimes overweening regard for the island home where he lived in later life, summed it up:

"London is, on the whole, the most possible form of life. I take it as an artist and a bachelor; as one who has the passion of observation and whose business is the study of human life. It is the biggest aggregation of human life—the most complete compendium of the world."

From the sacred to the profane: Amber St. Clare, the heroine of Kathleen Winsor's wildly successful 1945 Regency novel *Forever Amber,* concurs with James: "The memory of Newgate weighed on her like an incubus. But even more terrifying was the knowledge that if caught again she would very likely be either hanged or transported, and she was already so rabid a Londoner that one punishment seemed almost as bad as another."

For a person raised on books, walking through streets in her mind's eye, engaged in the love affairs and life losses of imaginary men and women, London is indisputably the capital of literature, of great literature and romance novels and mystery stories, too. There can be no doubt. The London of Thackeray and Galsworthy, of Martin and Kingsley Amis, of Margery Allingham and Dorothy Sayers, of Nancy Mitford and Elizabeth Bowen. The London of Conan Doyle, Oscar Wilde, and Charles Dickens.

This is not to say that all English literature takes place within the city. Some of the finest English novels are set in its quiet countryside—*Middlemarch, Tess of the D'Urbervilles, Wuthering Heights.* In *Pride and Prejudice,*

Kingsley Amis at home with his sons, Martin and Philip, in 1961

London is a metaphor for bad behavior and great unhappiness, where Jane Bennet is snubbed by the Bingley sisters and Lydia and Wickham go to ground after their ill-conceived elopement. And some of the greatest of all London novels portray it as a place of filthy back alleys and disreputable back rooms. The London of *Little Dorrit* is no tourist mecca, and Daniel Defoe's *Moll Flanders* spends most of her time in the streets of London fleeing from poverty and the police.

And that is only the novels. Some of the most riveting and most memorable stories in the true history of civilization come out of the city, from the wives of Henry VIII to the Great Fire of 1666 to the ascendancy of the young Victoria and the abdication of her great-grandson Edward VIII. The storeowners in the area all know that when a visitor with a notebook wanders through asking where Whitechapel is to be found, she is probably looking, not for the Royal London Hospital or the Bell Foundry, but for the haunts of Jack the Ripper, one of the first and still best-known serial killers.

On that first visit to London one of the first stops I made was in Westminster Abbey, at the catafalque of Elizabeth I; in my girlhood, before anyone used (and overused) the term "role model," that distant princess was mine, refusing to be demoted and undervalued because of her gender, determined to be the greatest ruler England had ever known and making a go of it, too. And, of course, there was the resting place of her mother, Anne Boleyn, up the Thames in the grounds of the Tower of London. What a story, that, as entrancing as any fairy tale or fable! Since I was a little girl, I have been able to recite the short history of Henry's six queens: divorced, beheaded, died, divorced, beheaded, survived.

If you have spent your days in an armchair with a book, your nights reading yourself to sleep, then London is the central character in so much of what you have read that it is as though it is your imaginary home, a place whose lineaments are as clear as those of your own living room despite the fact that—at least in my case—you have never set foot in the place. Because of time and circumstances, I did not actually go to London for the first time until that day when I was well into my forties, being put up at the Groucho Club so that I could promote one of my own books in the United Kingdom.

As I was set down in Soho by that disgruntled cabbie, I was not thinking of it as a neighborhood but as a series of word pictures. "You see it as you wish," P. D. James once wrote. "An agreeable place to dine; a cosmopolitan village tucked away behind Piccadilly with its own mysterious village life, one of the best shopping centers for food in London, the nastiest and most sordid nursery of crime in Europe." That was Adam Dalgliesh on Soho in *Unnatural Causes,* but there was also the Soho in which Robert and Stella stop for dinner on the way from the train station in Elizabeth Bowen's *The Heat of the Day,* the Soho about which John Galsworthy had written, in the trilogy about people of property and rigid propriety called *The Forsyte Saga,* "Of all the quarters in the queer adventurous amalgam called London, Soho is perhaps least suited to the Forsyte spirit. 'So-ho, my wild one!' George would have said if he had seen his cousin going there. Untidy, full of Greeks, Ishmaelites, cats, Italians, tomatoes, restaurants, organs, coloured stuffs, queer names, people looking out of upper windows, it dwells remote from the British Body Politic."

It seemed to me that morning that the area had not changed a bit. That made me very happy.

Perhaps it was that I wanted to see what I had learned, what I had read, what I had imagined, that I would never be able to see the city of London without seeing it through the overarching scrim of every description of it I had read before. When I turn the corner into a small, quiet, leafy square, am I really seeing it fresh, or am I both looking and remembering? Is it possible to stroll through Little Venice without having my perceptions colored by the artists in Margery Allingham's mystery novel *Death of a Ghost,* or to visit the Old Bailey without imagining John Mortimer's Rumpole trotting through its halls on his way from the cells to Pommeroy's Wine Bar for a glass of plonk? Can I ever shake the ghosts of Clarissa Dalloway and Dr. Johnson?

This is both the beauty and excitement of London, and its cross to bear, too. There is a tendency for visitors to turn the place into a theme park, the Disney World of social class, innate dignity, crooked streets, and grand houses, with a cavalcade of monarchs as varied and cartoony as Mickey Mouse, Snow White, and, at least in the opinion of various British broadsheets, Goofy.

They come, not to see what London is, or even what it was, but to confirm a kind of picture-postcard view of both, all red telephone kiosks and fog-wreathed alleyways.

As the tourists mass outside the gates of Buckingham Palace, also known as Buck House (or is that only what tourists who think they are au courant call it?), it is hard to conclude anything else. It is not only that the monarchy itself has become such a vestigial organ of the body politic in what is now a constitutional monarchy, but that this particular manifestation of its history and power is a kind of Potemkin village, neither illuminating nor majestic. ("A child with a box of bricks could have done better," one of the characters concludes of the palace architecture in Virginia Woolf's *Mrs. Dalloway.*)

The Foot Guards of the Household Regiment go through their famous change of personnel, in red coats and bearskin busbies, but the ordinary black-and-white coppers and the high security barriers around the old gilded palace gates tell the real story of the modern era. Down Birdcage Walk on a Saturday morning, in front of Wellington Barracks, two groups of guards, one with guns, one with drums, execute a complex pavane that is clearly as old as the Empire. But little is left of the Empire except a few stray Caribbean islands, the good-natured fealty of the Canadians, and the fact that, according to one cab driver, the second most common dinner dish in the U.K. (after roast beef and Yorkshire pudding) is chicken tikka masala.

It is difficult to watch all this without A. A. Milne's Christopher Robin rhyme going round and round in your head:

> *They're changing guard at Buckingham Palace—*
> *Christopher Robin went down with Alice.*
> *They've great big parties inside the grounds.*
> *"I wouldn't be King for a hundred pounds,"*
> *Says Alice.*

The guards with the musical instruments play the theme from *Austin Powers.* But is it really the theme from the silly cinematic satire of swinging England, or is it an ancient march tune co-opted by Hollywood producers? These are the sorts of questions that being an Anglophile tend to produce under the weight of long history and literary familiarity. Surely an American doesn't want to get it wrong; if there is anything that England stands for, with its quiet central squares, its tweeds and twin sets and teas, the tight-lipped precision of its speech, it is that there is a right way to do things. This is where the right way has its ancestral home.

"This is the past," said a British book editor, indicating the street scene outside a posh Knightsbridge restaurant with a languid hand, not long before he decamped for great success in New York. "America is the future."

An easy glib explanation for a shift in geopolitics that has taken place slowly, over centuries. But it is not entirely true. London has the trick of making its past, its long indelible incredible past, always a part of its present. And for that reason it will always have meaning for the future, because of all it can teach about disaster, survival, and redemption. It is all there in the streets. It is all there in the books.

CHAPTER THREE

L ondon opens to you like a novel itself. Those who
prefer Paris or Rome complain that the English
capital has no precise center, that there is no spot in
the city that could be considered the hub around
which the wheel revolves. There is some truth to that.
St. Paul's is an enormous visual marker from above,
like a stern presence looking down and around on all.
The string of parks—Hyde, Green, St. James's—make
a sort of central hub that enables newcomers to find
their way around some of the most important land-
marks and some of the prettiest neighborhoods.
Piccadilly Circus seems more important than it is

mainly because of the street bustle its tortured topo-graphical layout foments.

But the truth is that that is not really how London is apprehended. It is divided into chapters, the chapters into scenes, the scenes into sentences; it opens to you like a series of rooms, door, passage, door. Mayfair to Piccadilly to Soho to the Strand. Or, on a more intimate scale, the narrow little maze of Shepherd Market, with its ethnic restaurants and small spare trendy shops, to the wider but still quiet length of Curzon Street, to the full-on cacophony and traffic, both foot and auto, of Park Lane, and hence into the more quiet embrace of Hyde Park.

It is as though four different landscapes, histories, ways of living, can be encapsulated in a walk around the corner—almost any corner. One moment, the throng and the lowering office building. The next, quiet, isola-tion, and the window eyes of a mews house. London has nearly as many residents as New York has, yet even its most central locations never feel overwhelming in the way much of Manhattan does, mainly because of this effect, this ability to step within minutes from tumult into peace. In its variety—architectural, historical, top-ographical—London holds as unique and singular a place in the world as the glory of its literary legacy would suggest.

In *Howards End,* which despite being named for a country house is often a poetic, even elegiac tribute to the great city, E. M. Forster speaks of this:

"Their house was in Wickham Place, and fairly quiet, for a lofty promontory of buildings separated it from the main thoroughfare. One had the sense of a backwater, or rather of an estuary, whose waters flowed in from the invisible sea, and ebbed into a profound silence while the waves without were still beating. Though the promontory consisted of flats—expensive, with cavernous entrance halls, full of concierge and palms—it fulfilled its purpose, and gained for the older houses opposite a certain measure of peace."

Anyone who has passed from the busy Brompton Road to the lanes and streets behind it understands this description; it holds true over much of London, which is a city of neighborhoods, and within the neighborhoods a place of discreet areas, each with its own atmosphere, its own feeling, its own story. It is also a city of houses. All cities are, of course, but while other European capitals are most often thought of in terms of their grand public buildings—and Paris in terms of its pale apartment buildings, Rome its sun-colored palazzos wrapped around an atrium of garden—the essential London scene is a row of low identical houses set around a square.

Many, if not most, London novels are set in such single-family buildings, upstairs and down. It took me a long time to figure out that the terrace house I encountered in so many novels is what we in the United States call a row house, in New York, no matter its material, a brownstone. (It also took me a long time to figure out that the council flats on estates that made an appearance in many modern novels were not grand places to live. They certainly didn't *sound* like public housing projects. Bedsits, on the other hand, were pretty self-explanatory.)

London is also a city of parks, gardens, and squares, so that much more of it is green and verdant than visitors initially suspect. (A third of London, according to one estimate, is grass or gardens. "Nothing to see but streets, streets, streets," writes Dickens in *Little Dorrit.* "Nothing to breathe but streets, streets, streets." But that was only in Southwark, around the debtors' prisons.) Whole blocks of London in the springtime smell rich and musky; while a stroller moves in minutes from bustle to quiet, she may also pass through successive waves of perfume, lilacs, roses, syringa, even the stew-like scent of good rich loamy soil. A reader understands this coming into the city for the first time simply because so much of the action of so many novels has taken place in these hidden spots, only steps from busy roads, in the squares and parks. Eaton Square. Regent's Park. They have come to have a mellifluous, slightly mysterious sound, even though in reality they prove to be more ordinary than their names. They could easily be the titles of books, not simply their settings.

"I love walking in London," says the title character of Virginia Woolf's *Mrs. Dalloway,* perhaps the perfect twentieth-century London novel. "Really it's better than walking in the country." When the destitute protagonist of Trollope's *The Prime Minister* is in despair and deciding on a course of action, he walks the streets of London, despite nasty weather: "He went round by Trafalgar Square, and along the Strand, and up some dirty streets by the small theaters, and so on to Holborn and by Bloomsbury Square up to Tottenham Court Road, then through some unused street into Portland Place, along the Marylebone Road, and back to Manchester Square by Baker Street." Unlike cities that have been modernized, renovated, changed, a visitor could walk precisely this walk today, including those "dirty streets by the small theaters," and wind up as Ferdinand Lopez eventually does, at the great junction where trains go in and out of London. From there, onto the tracks.

Of course, walking in London frequently includes getting lost in London, even for some longtime residents.

A city first founded in Roman times and eventually encompassing a string of outlying villages has streets that could, most kindly, be classified as organic. In other words, once upon a time they were cow paths and the crossroads stiles. Any reader of Dickens knows the maze of narrow back streets that enables pickpockets to melt into a crowd and young orphans to disappear without a trace, ideal "for the very purpose of concealment," wrote Henry Fielding, the author of *Tom Jones*. Any reader of history knows how stubbornly Londoners have held onto a street grid that seems to have been based on the children's printed puzzles of trying to get from one side of a square to another. "Right lines have hardly ever been considered," complained an architect in 1766. For a writer, of course, this polyglot landscape is irresistible, right lines not being the purview of the novelist or poet.

CHAPTER FOUR

One of the most exciting things about the city of London is how it honors those who labor in the salt mines of words. The most obvious manifestation of this is what is called Poet's Corner in Westminster Abbey. The truth is that the poets are somewhat edged out by the prose writers, and the corner is more a large anteroom, crowded with gawkers by virtue of its notoriety, relatively spacious compared with the rooms on the other side of the aisle simply because there are no recumbent kings or archbishops in this neck of the abbey. To arrive at Poet's Corner in this age of pragmatism, it is now, unfortunately, necessary to thread your way through a maze of assorted barriers and one-way signs: "For the sake of moving it along, madam," one of the red-robed marshals says.

(In England I am always madam; I arrived too late to ever be a miss. In New York I have only been madamed once, by the doorman at the Carlyle Hotel.)

The assortment of writers is various, the feeling ecstatic: So here they all are! Chaucer, Dryden, Browning, Tennyson, Byron, Dickens, of course, and even Noel Coward, his plaque beneath the doleful monument to two sisters who died in the early eighteenth century and distinctly at odds with it, with the unfunereal legend "A Talent to Amuse."

Very few of the writers are actually buried with the monarchs in the abbey, and more modern plaques reflect that: George Eliot, Mary Ann Evans, buried at Highgate, and Dylan Thomas, buried at Laugharne. Henry James is there with his divided literary loyalties: "New York, 1843; London, 1916." And Dickens has a large plain black slab in the floor with simply his name, the brass as shiny as if it had just been polished, perhaps by thousands of fingers, or feet.

Although London book editors today are every bit as pessimistic and lachrymose about sales as their American counterparts, it is still possible to believe, at moments like this, that this island, and this city, are indeed the ancestral home of literature. The Underground stations are full of enormous posters for the latest blockbuster. The newspapers cover publishing thoroughly, although not as thoroughly as sport, the monarchy, and the current reigning reality television show. There are eight daily papers, many more than any American city has—even if several seem devoted more to photographs of women's breasts and coverage of the unsavory sexual pasts of contestants in the television show "Big Brother"—and many of them cover the book business as though it were a spectator sport. On one spring Sunday alone there were articles about a bookstore in Mayfair, a book festival in Wales, the writer Mary Wesley, the writer Patricia Highsmith, as well as the usual reviews and publishing news.

The bookstore in Mayfair, a journalist reports, has stayed alive despite the fact that it sells both new and used books from a spot on Curzon Street that (like so much else in London) is a challenge for a visitor to locate. The clerks know longtime customers by name and taste; one elderly lady, the newspaper story recounts, was once prepared to buy a gardening book for a peeress and was told apologetically by the manager, "I'm afraid she already has it." In an age when most bookstore trade seems to be more like buying blue jeans than buying words, this sounds more than a little like a

Curzon Street

place in a novel. This, in some transmuted form, it likely has been, since in *The Pursuit of Love* Nancy Mitford's heroine works in a bookstore (albeit one identified as on a "slummy little street," which Curzon Street has never been), and a small oval plaque on the outside of the G. Heywood Hill shop identifies it as a place in which Mitford herself once worked. Thus London becomes a hall of mirrors: real shop, real writer, imagined shop, imagined shopgirl. It's commonplace to talk of the autobiographical novel. London is also the home of the autogeographical one.

Nearly every block in the center of the city seems to have at least one building with one of these small oval blue enamel plaques identifying some great literary enterprise that has taken place within. Granted, some of those plaques honor statesman, as politicians are called in England when they are dead, or long retired. Disraeli, Charles Fox. But the lion's share are memorials to writers. One is attached to a narrow house at 46 Gordon Street, which is now the office of career services for the University of London. "Here and in the neighboring houses during the first half of the 20th century," it reads, in somewhat wordier fashion than is usual, "there lived several members of the Bloomsbury Group, including Virginia Woolf, Clive Bell and the Stracheys."

For readers and writers who came of age in the middle of the twentieth century, the word "Bloomsbury" carries weight that perhaps cries out for a plaque wordier than the run-of-the-mill. Woolf and her friends were in the act of trying something entirely different: in their lives, their work, their relationships, their relationship with the world. The plaque is a little misleading in its specificity; biographies of the Woolfs make clear that they hopscotched all over the area, from one prettily named backwater to another—Gordon Square, Fitzroy Square, Brunswick Square, Tavistock Square. Enemy bombing in Mecklenburgh Square during the Second World War drove them permanently into the country and the famous rendezvous with the river and the stones in her pocket that now seem the inevitable denouement of Virginia's mental illness.

The choice of neighborhood by the Woolfs and their circle makes clear what any reader knows about London: that geography is destiny. It is one of the central tenets of English literature: Where you live tells us who you are, or who you have become, or want to be. Not simply what sort of house you occupy, but what street it stands in. When the Sedleys move from Russell Square, with its tall distinguished houses and the long drawing room windows overlooking the trees and the gravel paths, to what is described as a "baby house" near the Fulham

Road in Thackeray's *Vanity Fair,* it is immediately clear even to those who have never visited either place that their family fortunes have plummeted. On the other hand, in Trollope's *The Prime Minister,* the compromised and questionable Lady Eustace "lived in a very small house in a very small street bordering upon Mayfair, but the street, though very small, and having disagreeable relation with a mews, still had an air of fashion about it." When the heroine of Nancy Mitford's novel *The Pursuit of Love* leaves Bryanston Square, and her husband, for a small house on the Thames at the end of Cheyne Walk, she has exchanged an advantageous marriage for the life of a freewheeling freethinker. ("The worst of being a Communist is that the parties you may go to are—well—awfully funny and touching but not very gay," she tells her sister.)

So it was that the Woolfs chose an area pretty, solid, clearly respectable but with an edge of bohemianism. Londoners to the bone, the members of the Bloomsbury group knew that they would be making a statement about intellectualism and individualism (and perhaps free love and sexual experimentation) merely by putting their address on their writing paper. Writes Virginia's nephew Nigel Nicolson, "It was a district of London that, in spite of the elegance of its Georgian squares, was considered by Kensington to be faintly decadent, the resort

Gandhi's statue, Tavistock Square

34   ANNA QUINDLEN

of raffish divorcées and indolent students, loose in its morals and behaviour."

In short, it seemed the ideal spot for writers, then and now. In Tavistock Square today, for instance, the focal point is a statue of Gandhi, a clutch of votive candles at the base of the memorial, a branch of flowers habitually wilting in his cross-legged lap. To one side of him is a tree "planted in memory of the victims of Hiroshima by the worshipful mayor of Camden councillour Mrs. Millie Miller JP 6 August 1967," and not far from it is an enormous slab of rock littered with browning white carnations with the inscription "To all those who have established and are maintaining the right to refuse to kill," which turns out to be a memorial to conscientious objectors. Nothing could be less Hyde Park Gate, the stuffy upper class neighborhood Virginia and her sister sought to escape by fleeing a few miles to Bloomsbury.

CHAPTER FIVE

Hyde Park Gate is, instead, the nexus of Forsyte land. For years the novels by John Galsworthy were out of fashion, despite an improbable Nobel Prize for Literature for their author. But two excellent television productions produced new paperback versions and a boom in sales. Nothing could improve the opinion of the literati—the English literary critic V. S. Pritchett, with his usual high-handed harshness, describes the author's imagination as "lukewarm," and *The Forsyte Saga* is relentlessly described by English literary critics as "middlebrow," the English literary equivalent of acid in the face—but a new generation of readers discovered this family saga, and discovered that while it is not *Middlemarch* it is nonetheless quite entertaining and often moving. It is also a book in which London features almost mathematically as a map of the fortunes, aspirations, limitations, and adaptations of its various characters.

I'm not sure if anyone has ever put together a Forsyte's tour of London, although having been handed innumerable flyers for several Dickens one-man shows, a Sherlock Holmes impersonation, and a look at the phony London Dungeon that has been staged as a kind of quasihistorical amusement park ride, I wouldn't be at all surprised. It is the perfect tourist novel, in some sense, since so much of it is about what people own, what it says about them, and how their lives appear from the outside. In other words, real estate and facades.

It is possible to organize a tour yourself, somewhat in the manner of the "Good Walk" section of a Fodor's guidebook that loops around what were once called "the fashionable ways." It's also possible to be struck immediately by how little has changed, and how much, which, of course, is the keynote of London. Galsworthy draws a little map in words, early on in this doorstop of a book, confident, it's clear, that his readers will understand the code contained in the addresses: "There was old Jolyon in Stanhope Place; the James in Park Lane; Swithin in the lonely glory of orange and blue chambers in Hyde Park Mansions—he had never married, not he!—the Soamses in their nest in Knightsbridge, the Rogers in Princes Gardens."

They are all still there, 150 years after the action of the novel: the tall houses with the white fronts and the dignified columns, the street where Swithin lived, with its buffer of old-growth trees from the busy traffic of the Bayswater Road. But Park Lane was savaged in the early part of the last century, the bowfront houses with gardens running right down to the edge of the greensward largely demolished and the road along Hyde Park widened into a major autobahn. The broad avenue is a hodgepodge now: of lovely old houses taken hostage by corporations and equipped with security keypads to one side of the fanlit doors and sleek office furniture as out of place as a cow in the high-ceilinged parlors; of graceless apartment blocks with postage stamp balconies scarcely worthy of the name and certainly not capable of a chair and a table from which to sit and savor the view; of estate agents offering more of the same; of Jaguar and Rolls-Royce dealerships.

In the park itself is a posted timeline, showing how it too has changed, the land acquired by Henry VIII for hunting in 1536, hangings at Tyburn discontinued in 1783. There is a notice on the board to leave the baby birds alone: "Parent birds rear their young better than you can." Another asks for public help with information on a recent assault and carries the heading RAPE in red capital letters. A third suggests the number of dogs that can reasonably be handled by a single park-goer (four) but concludes that no hard-and-fast rule will be made "at this time." Young Londoners seem a bit sick of the stereotypical view of the English: doggy bird-watchers mired in propriety and history. It is just that the stereotype seems to so often conform to observable reality.

It is probably in the London parks that the descriptions contained within its best known novels come most alive; it is also in the parks that a reader realizes that the London frozen in the amber of great fiction is a London quite out-of-date and out of time. The soldiers on horseback in Rotten Row may seem more appropriate than the runners in shorts and singlets simply because, for a reader, the tableau of Hyde Park is indelibly one of a parade of conveyances, barouche and phaeton and curricle. (I have encountered them all dozens of times in period fiction. I still have no idea what they are, much as after all these years of reading the English magazine *Tatler* I have still not managed to puzzle out who gets to be called an Honorable, and why. Frankly, I don't much care.) The milky-skinned English roses are outnumbered by Indian families walking with their sloe-eyed children. This is part of the problem with developing an understanding of London simply from reading its great books; too much of it takes place in the eighteenth and nineteenth centuries, too little in the present, on buses and the Underground and in the back of an Austin Mini and in neighborhoods rich with the sounds and smells of India or Jamaica.

Surely there are still Becky Sharps, manipulating their way into an advantageous marriage and a lucrative lifestyle; the British magazines are full of them, in towering heels and dwindling skirts. But seeing Hyde Park through the eyes of a Forsyte is as ridiculous as seeing Greenwich Village through the eyes of Henry James. The modern, the ever changing, insists on tapping you on the shoulder or, occasionally, slapping you in the face. In the Princes Gardens block where the Roger Forsytes once set up housekeeping, there are indeed the expected elegant white houses with small pillared porticos. But at the corner is the half-sunken modern block that is the sports center of the Imperial College of Science, Technology and Medicine, "pilates classes, inquire within." And, across the square, a kind of Soviet gray structure sits as the antidote to the slender lightness of the older houses; it must be a dormitory, for only college students use flags as curtains. The students fly across the square on bicycles and the occasional skateboard or pair of Rollerblades; if Soames Forsyte was appalled at his daughter's necklines, he should see the young women with pierced navels moving hither and yon.

In fact, he was appalled long before the twentieth century had given over to the twenty-first: "A democratic England," he concludes bitterly by the end of the saga. "Disheveled, hurried, noisy and seemingly without an apex.... Gone forever, the close borough of rank and polish." Every British generation has complained that its successor has transgressed the old standards. One of London's best known poems is a version of the kind of not-what-it-used-to-be that you can hear creaking out of the old hands at any pub. In this case the old hand happens to be Wordsworth:

> Milton! Thou should'st be living at this hour:
> England hath need of thee: she is a fen
> Of stagnant waters: altar, sword, and pen,
> Fireside, the heroic wealth of hall and bower,
> Have forfeited their ancient English dower
> Of inward happiness. We are selfish men;
> Oh! Raise us up, return to us again ...

Or, as the cabbie on his way to Islington said as he frowned at a brace of Indian students on bicycles, his complaint at one with the spirit of Soames and Wordsworth both, "The city isn't what it was, miss, I can tell you that." The jeremiad that followed about the effects of immigration on the economy, the crime rate, and unemployment was as old as time, and as literature.

Galsworthy is a better novelist than he is given credit for, and he chooses his settings well. Soames's sister Winifred lives in a house in Green Street rented for her and her husband Montague, who gambles and womanizes. Green Street is a pleasant and quiet lane off the park, and anyone would be pleased to own one of the houses that line it. But they are markedly less grand than those of the elder Forsytes, clearly the right place for a female child who has married a man of little fortune and uncertain reputation. These are buildings slighter, less chesty, more burgher than baron.

Property is, after all, what the saga is about, and what so many English novels, particularly of the nineteenth century, find of greatest concern. (Galsworthy, like Edith Wharton, is a twentieth-century man who appears to have been becalmed a century before his time.) Americans confuse this with class, since they like to think of themselves as members of a classless society, just as they like to think of their British counterparts as hopelessly immured in a hierarchy hatched a millennium ago. Neither is accurate. It is a mistake to make too much of democracy, or aristocracy. The great fulcrum is industry. At the end of the third book of the Forsyte saga, there is a society wedding at which the family takes pride in the inability to distinguish between themselves, landed bourgeoisie, and the titled family with whom they were now allied. "Was there, in the crease of his trousers, the expression of his moustache, his accent or the shine on his top hat, a pin to choose between Soames and the ninth baronet himself?" they ask in one narrative voice.

(Or there is this, in a more satirical vein, from *Vile Bodies,* one of Evelyn Waugh's hilarious and beautifully mean-spirited satires: "At Archie Schwert's party the fifteenth Marquess of Vanburgh, Earl Vanburgh de Brendon, Baron Brendon, Lord of the Five Isles and Hereditary Grand Falconer to the Kingdom of Connaught, said to the eighth Earl of Balcairn, Viscount Erdinge, Baron Cairn of Balcairn, Red Knight of Lancaster, Count of the Holy Roman Empire and Chenonceaux Herald to the Duchy of Aquitaine, 'Hullo,' he said. 'Isn't this a repulsive party? What are you going to say about it?' for they were both of them, as it happened, gossip writers for the daily papers." So much for title in the twentieth century.)

This is apparent in the park, too, in the democratization of place and of fashion. No more are the gentry discernible from their servants by the cut of a jacket, the curl of a wig, the impeccable handle of the right umbrella or briefcase. Japanese tourists conspicuously carry expensive leather bags, while the young English princes are seen in blue jeans and university sweatshirts. Nannies dress as well as the mothers they so closely resemble. No great city will ever be without strata, London perhaps least of all. But they are more difficult to define than ever before.

It was this that Soames lamented when he decried a democratic England, this ability to tell a gentleman by the notch of his lapel. By the time Soames's daughter Fleur is married, he is living outside of the city, some ways from the house in Knightsbridge where the story begins. Number 62, Montpelier Square, it says, is where he begins his ill-fated marriage to the alluring Irene, who feels suffocated by her husband and their life together. And, to be sure, Montpelier Square even today feels hermetically sealed, although it is only a few blocks from Harrods and the busy Brompton Road. The garden at its center, with its carefully manicured wall of hedges and tidy gravel paths, can easily be

Montpelier Square

imagined as a cross between a sanctuary and a green prison. Wisteria vines climb the walls of several of the houses, giving them a sort of *Sleeping Beauty* quality. At midafternoon on a workaday weekday, there is no one in the central garden, no one on the square, no one on the streets at all except for two workmen working on the pointing of an exquisitely restored house, a hint of lavish drape and bullion trim just visible through the long windows.

Like many of the most beautiful squares in Knightsbridge and Belgravia, Montpelier Square has the trick of seeming as distant from the push and pull and press of the main roads as if it had a great glass skylit ceiling over it. It is possible to imagine either being completely content here, or very very restless. Or perhaps that is just remembering the novel, remembering Irene and her discontent.

Round and round the square, peering at the house numbers for 62, where Soames kept her like an especially beautiful painting in a frame of crystal and polished furniture. Round and round again. But there is no number 62. Perhaps the author wanted to protect any actual house from the taint that might attach to the fictional unhappiness in his own creation. Perhaps he chose a number out of the air, without any attention to the house numbers on Montpelier Square itself. Perhaps in a small way he wanted to drive home what is always a valuable lesson, when we insist on learning the world through books: that accuracy and truth are sometimes quite different things.

CHAPTER SIX

My excitement, even joy in the concrete existence of these fictional locations—even if the numbers don't exactly match—raises an obvious question. Why did I wait so long to visit London in the first place? Like every American teenager, I'd had my chance to backpack through Europe, an excursion that inevitably included a hostel in Chelsea, a pub near Piccadilly, and far too much Guinness. "Another pint!" friends of mine shrieked in a private joke when they'd returned. "Please, sir—I want some more."

I suppose that was part of it, that feeling of being the ugly American in the high reaches of high art that

Jane Austen, 1775-1817

made me cringe. It is a sense I experience each time I return to London about the essential character of its people: They are cordial strangers, happy to proffer directions, say, but content then to be on their way without the sort of where-you-from-how-you-like-it pleasantries that would be the hallmark of any such American exchange. As an experiment I once stood on a corner of the Strand with an open map and a pronounced expression of confusion for fifteen minutes. I can assure you that if I did this on Broadway someone would offer directions, since New Yorkers are indefatigable know-it-alls. In London, not a single passerby volunteered.

This national character is quite clear after only a few days in London, and clearer still in fiction. Those who chatter or openly emote are classified in virtually all English novels as fools; in fact, the mindless yammerer, fecklessly easy with strangers and unthinking of propriety, is a bit of a stock character, the best known version being Mrs. Bennet in *Pride and Prejudice*. When Londoners do become what, in the parlance of their national character, might be considered overwrought (although certainly not by any passersby in New York), it is usually because of something flagrantly un-English. So it was that, in the fall of 2003, city residents responded savagely to the American David Blaine. Blaine is usually referred to as an "illusionist," which is what you call a magician with pretensions and a press agent, and for reasons obscure he decided to spend forty-four days in a Plexiglas box suspended from a crane near Tower Bridge.

This was originally described heroically as a feat, like Blaine's feats in America, where he was encased in a block of ice and a coffin and lionized while doing so. But the English perceived this sort of display not as a feat, but as a stunt. And because they are a people who decry unwarranted spectacle—they are, after all, the subjects of a queen who, when not wearing the Crown Jewels and an ermine cloak, often has on enormous rubber boots—they took after the American. During his time in the box, Blaine was pelted with eggs, golf balls, and loud opprobrium.

Perhaps it was in part because Blaine had set his plastic box up over the Thames, a bit like a monument on a plinth by the shores of what is, in many ways, less a river than the single most indelible piece of British history. Birdcage Walk has been paved over since Charles II rode his horse down its length, and the reading room of the British Museum has a new roof and new books. But there is something about flowing water that seems immutable, as though there might still be a hint of Cromwell or Chaucer running beneath the bridges, the most eternal part of a constantly reconstituted city. "Sweet Thames, run softly, till I end my song," Edmund Spenser wrote in the sixteenth century, and then T. S. Eliot added to it four centuries later:

> *Sweet Thames, run softly, till I end my song.*
> *The river bears no empty bottles, sandwich papers,*
> *Silk handkerchiefs, cardboard boxes, cigarette ends*
> *Or other testimony of summer nights.*

The London newspapers suggested that Blaine's rude welcome was a function of class warfare or anti-Americanism. But perhaps it would have been different had he not set himself up over London's great living monument, the longest river in Britain. His stunt became the modern equivalent of a public hanging, with the crane giving a gallowslike air to the enterprise. When Blaine was tormented by the sound of drums from below, and the hurling of French fries, perhaps he ought to have been grateful; Thackeray went to a hanging once at which the dandies squirted the crowd from upper windows with brandy and soda, and sometimes after the body had been taken down sections of the rope would be sold as souvenirs.

Perhaps it was simply that Blaine seemed literally and figuratively to have gotten above his station, to be openly boastful in a way the British find repellent. The Londoners who are effusive seem to be so as an act, usually for profit: the cab drivers, the souvenir hawkers, those who offer bus tours and maps on the busier street corners. (Either that, or they are hosting game shows on television. If he were writing today, Dickens would doubtless have Mr. Micawber introducing humiliating snippets from home videos with a laugh track playing madly.) Many of them seem to have taken a page from *The Pickwick Papers* or the musical *Oliver!* and the result is not a happy one, a bit like that overamped tour of the London Dungeon.

In the way that the Dutch are blunt and businesslike, the Italians warm and gregarious, and the French high-handed, the men and women of London seem to be by nature reserved. In nineteenth-century novels this is frequently portrayed as a division of class—the wealthy are reserved out of snobbery, the lower classes outgoing and therefore democratic—but in actual modern life the sense of standing apart from strangers seems to span social and economic class. Perhaps it reflects a kind of triumph: Londoners, after all, have prevailed, prevailed over epidemics and economic downturns, foreign enemies and pesky tourists. They need not stoop to empty pleasantry. This reserve is even reflected in the most recognizable of English architecture, the terrace house: Those long graceful rows of identical buildings, standing foursquare to the street, give nothing away about the lives inside except, perhaps, that on some cosmetic level they are lives well lived. They hold their peace.

I, on the other hand, do not. I am an almost pathologically extroverted person even by United States standards—the operative cliché in America is "she never met a stranger"—and in London, more than any place on Earth, it seemed to me that this would be akin to having a particularly glaring birth defect.

I never spoke of that, however, when the surprising fact arose that I had never been to London. (Never been abroad, actually. Too, too shamemaking, as Nina Blount would have it in *Vile Bodies*.) It was always that I had a newspaper job whose various duties made a transatlantic trip impossible. But even when I was given the opportunity to cover the wedding of the Lady Diana Spencer to his Royal Highness the Prince of Wales—which, for a certain sort of female reporter of my generation, was like covering the World Series or the splitting of the atom—I found some excuse to let the assignment go to another reporter, someone who knew from past experience how to negotiate the streets around St. Paul's Cathedral. Even without the knowledge of foresight, without knowing that the event was not only the world's most closely watched nuptials but a kind of literary festival of sorts, since the marriage would wind up covering the gamut from Grimm's *Fairy Tales* to an Evelyn Waugh satire to a kind of unholy John Osborne play of regret, betrayal, and recrimination, saying no to the royal wedding suggested that avoiding London had become as much of a personal avocation as reading about it had long been.

It did not take psychoanalysis to figure out that a large part of this was the fear of disappointment. From the earliest days of our family, when it was only my husband and me, before our children joined in, we had read aloud from *A Christmas Carol* each Christmas Eve. Critics can say what they will about Dickens, and they are often right; he does sometimes seem as though he were staging a crazed Punch and Judy show on the village green of the mind rather than writing a novel, certainly any sort of naturalistic one. But if you read his work aloud as a kind of performance, as he did on his reading tours, there is no doubt that he creates a world.

In *A Christmas Carol,* a slight book whose cachet has been further depleted by its incarnation as, among other things, a Muppet movie and a musical extravaganza at Madison Square Garden in New York, that world is almost tangible. That London, too. It is a cold night, and powerfully foggy, and a group of the poor are gathered around a fire, and carolers go from door to door. In one warehouse the workers are dancing into the night, with a fiddler playing along with the help of a pint of porter. In a small house a poor family is eating every morsel of goose. In a larger one a young couple and their friends are playing at Blindman's Bluff. And at the end, Scrooge the ogre is "as good a man as the good old city knew," which is as good a way as saying "happily ever after" as any. By the time they were six my children could recite some of this from memory, and by the time they were twelve they had laid claim to the chapter, or stave, that they would read each year. Ask any of them what "a bad lobster in a dark cellar" describes (the spectral face of Marley glowing on Scrooge's doorknocker), and they can tell you.

At a time when England in general and London specifically were dealing with modern urban evils, with bad health care, high unemployment, domestic terrorism, anti-immigration bigotry, and increasing crime, the fact that there would be no lamplighters nor poulterer's shops seems a most pathetic reason for an educated woman, particularly one who also happened to be a reporter and a writer, to stay away from that place that, above all else, called her home. This was wacky, and it was quite specific: I am a Philadelphian by birth and have visited the Liberty Bell and Independence Hall many times, and not once have I felt rattled or bereft by the fact that I was unlikely to meet Benjamin Franklin on Rittenhouse Square. (On the other hand, there are precious few great novels set in Philadelphia.) Yet so it was with London. Each of us has an illusion we would prefer to maintain intact. The Vatican, the Far East, the Grand Canyon, Hollywood. (Truly an illusion, that last one.) This was mine.

What a relief to discover, on that first visit, that on close acquaintance I loved London rather more than less, as much for what she had become as what she had

been, although the two seemed to me to be insepara-
ble. Although I had work to do—interviews in the
back of the Groucho's slightly lugubrious dining
room, afternoons at Broadcasting House, from which
the BBC seems to have what any American journalist
would consider a stranglehold on the media—my free
time was spent wandering aimlessly through the
streets of London, from Covent Garden through the
West End, along the Strand and down to the Thames.
Listening to the half-slurry, half-sharp intonations of
the average English accent, passing a group of suited
city types ranged outside the crammed entryway of a
pub, taking the vertiginous escalators down into the
Underground and then up again, all while moving
from monument to monument—it was just as I'd
imagined, and then some.

All around was the city I had learned to know, in all
its incarnations. There were the street beggars with
their dogs tucked into doorways. There were the
lawyers—solicitors and barristers, I hadn't learned to
tell the difference, and QCs, I suppose, whatever that
may be—moving like guided missiles in pinstripes to
and from the Inns of Court. There were the giddy rich
girls looking through the racks on Beauchamp Place in
South Kensington, a clutch of nannies with their
charges in strollers in Hyde Park, a young man in

paint-streaked overalls selling river scenes next to the boats that take tourists up and down the Thames. There was a new London, a real London, a London apart from anything I had read that told its own stories through overheard conversations, glimpses into shop windows, bored faces on the train, waitresses in Soho coffeehouses.

The guard had changed.

I love big cities, find New York warm and companionable, think a little of the country goes a long way. So I loved this London from the very first precisely because past and present coexisted so completely. I would not say happily, always, since as a closet antiquarian I often find offensive the way in which the modern too often seems intent on shoving aside, with a big boxy hip, the slender graceful remnants of its own history. Perhaps nowhere was I as struck by this as I was in the City, for quickly I learned that that locution in literature referred not, as I had supposed, to the city of London, but to the part of London that is the oldest and today most dedicated to finance and commerce. It happened as I came upon the monument to the Great Fire of London. The denizens of the area had been wiped out by the Great Plague in 1665, and their chockablock little houses, shanties really, by a ravenous fire in 1666, and to commemorate the devastation Christopher Wren—whose contributions to the architecture of London in sheer number suggest that he never slept nor ate sitting down—conceived of a great stone column, erected not far from the baking house in Pudding Lane from which the flames were said to have first erupted and spread. Atop the pillar is a crown of flames, and at its base the explanation that the fire "consumed more than 13,000 houses and devastated 436 acres."

What's devastated, however, is the majesty of the monument, which was designed to be seen by anyone crossing London Bridge from the south bank of the Thames. Now it is a little like finding a needle, not in a haystack, but in a box of blocks, the large ungainly office towers around it, including that monument to the spread of American capitalism, the London headquarters of Merrill Lynch. And at the Tower of London, where I squatted in awe on the green at a sign explaining that Anne Boleyn's bones were beneath the ground nearby, I was amazed to see that the ravens that once picked at the heads on pikes at Tower Bridge were still in residence, then a bit dispirited to discover that their wings were clipped so that they could stay within the Tower close in their now purely ornamental capacity. St. Paul's Cathedral has a revolving door for the convenience of the tourists and the staff; nearby is a pleasant Japanese restaurant, the only place in the financial district open for lunch on a Saturday. Thus did I make my peace with modernism, as most of us do, through convenience. Over sushi I read *Scoop!* and thus mollified myself with tall tales of Fleet Street within walking distance of the place itself.

CHAPTER SEVEN

Not too far from Fleet Street, in that part of Bloomsbury near to Gray's Inn, there is a street without the feeling of insulation and isolation the Forsytes must have had in Montpelier Square. Even its name takes it down a peg from Pall Mall or nearby Mecklenburgh Square: Doughty Street. History tells us that there were once porter's lodges at either end, and gates that were closed and locked at night, creating an oasis within the bustle of the area. But there is none of that now. Rows of identical houses peer at one another from across a fairly busy avenue. None stands out from the others except that there is one that has a sandwich board on the sidewalk inviting passersby inside.

Of all the writers who have made London their palette, their paint, their turf and their home, Charles Dickens is the gargantua. Inside the Doughty Street house it is clear that it has always been so, although this was where he lived before his assumed greatness became monumental and his public readings became as popular as public hangings had once been. The memorabilia that has been assembled by The Dickens Fellowships, whose members around the world take Dickens as seriously as the Archbishop of Canterbury takes Jesus, cover the full range of a career that spanned thirty-five years and included, among other works, *David Copperfield, Oliver Twist, Bleak House,* and *A Tale of Two Cities.* (A rabid Dickensian—and is there any other kind?—I cannot bear to leave it at that. There is also *Little Dorrit, Dombey and Son, Nicholas Nickleby,* and *A Christmas Carol.*)

Until the publication of the Harry Potter books, Dickens may well have been the British writer most often read by American schoolchildren, usually because his work was assigned to them. He is also largely responsible for a kind of back-alley view of London that prevails to the present day. Although literary critics tend to treat him a little like a happy fantabulist and a talented hack—"Dickens could never have written such a passage," Oxford professor John Carey writes dismissively, quoting Thackeray approvingly in an introduction to an edition of *Vanity Fair*—his view of London, if not its people, is often astonishingly dark.

Along with some of the more florid detective novelists and the song "A Foggy Day In London Town," written by the American George Gershwin, Dickens may be singlehandedly responsible for the common perception that the weather may frequently render London's streets so impassable as to be impossible. In the very beginning of *Bleak House,* after introducing mud so deep that prehistoric creatures might still be expected to be crawling out of the ooze, he continues, with the lack of restraint that is his hallmark, "Fog everywhere. Fog up the river, where it flows among green aits and meadows; fog down the river where it rolls defiled among the tiers of shipping and the waterside pollutions of a great (and dirty) city." And so on and on in a paragraph that contains the word "fog" thirteen times, as well as five semicolons.

I may have been blessed in terms of timing, but I haven't encountered the kind of weather that has become the ruling London cliché. Instead, I've always been charmed by the light, which seems to me to have a silver-gilt quality that renders the atmosphere serious and expectant. I love that golden, almost edible light in Italy and the French Riviera, but it seems to me the meteorological opposite number of deep thoughts. London weather—the chill spring, the light rain, the dove-gray sky—telegraphs moments of moment and the tramp-tramp of real life. And I have never encountered much of an English fog, and certainly not the sort of pernicious blanket of dirty black that Dickens delights in describing.

The passage always recalls to me my first run-in with the notion that Dickens was a bit of a blowhard. When I brought home *Oliver Twist* in my book bag, assigned to read it in seventh grade (a terrible idea, as though within our suburban, center-hall colonials we twelve-year-olds would naturally relate to the prepubescent Oliver as he was orphaned, lost, and steered toward a life of crime), my mother commiserated with me about the rigors of reading Dickens. "He describes every leaf on every tree in every street in every town," she said.

This is a pretty fair assessment of the sort of detail the writer piles on (and which detractors assign to the fact that he was filling magazine pages, since many of his books were first serialized), but it so happened that I was a leaf-tree-street-town sort of person and, later, the same sort of writer. And there was something about the chapter I had read surreptitiously in the classroom, during (I'm pretty sure) a lesson on oblique and obtuse angles, that had simply gotten to me. It was the moment of the orphan's birth: "There was considerable difficulty in inducing Oliver to take upon himself the office of respiration." It was a combination of the arch and the archaic that spoke to me. Perhaps it was all those years reading the simple serviceable prose of the New Testament in Catholic school; I was dying for something with some potatoes and two veg along with the meat.

From his perch in the comfortable Victorian starter house that has now become a museum to his genius—dining room, morning room, drawing room, dressing room, but not much room for servants—Dickens created an indelible London in novels that merged storytelling with social commentary. But the fog was the least of it. One word-picture of an area near St. Paul's by the Thames in *Little Dorrit* describes "an old brick house, so dingy as to be all but black, standing by itself within a gateway. Before it, a square courtyard where a shrub or two and a patch of grass were as rank (which is saying much) as the iron railings enclosing them were rusty; behind it, a jumble of roots." Oliver Twist finds himself living with Fagin in rooms in which "the mouldering shutters were fast closed: the bars which held them were

Charles Dickens during his visit to the United States in 1867-68

screwed tight into the wood, the only light which was admitted, stealing its way through round holes at the top, which made the rooms more gloomy and filled them with strange shadows." A visitor can take the Tube to London's most notorious neighborhoods, and not see anything that approaches the dingy squalor of Dickens's London. This is either a tribute to urban renewal or literary overstatement.

Unsurprisingly, many of the books grew out of autobiography. The Dickens who was put to work labeling bottles in a blacking factory is mirrored in *David Copperfield.* The boy whose father was sent to debtors' prison, along with his entire family, grew up to reflect the experience in *Little Dorrit.* And the months he spent in the office of a firm of Gray's Inn attorneys informed the intractable litigation Jarndyce v. Jarndyce, the suit at the center of *Bleak House* that has made it the essential novel about the grinding inexorability of the self-perpetuating legal systems of all nations.

In the Doughty Street house there is a rather famous painting of Dickens by R. W. Buss, who was one of the original illustrators of *The Pickwick Papers.* It shows the familiar figure—for it is a measure of Dickens's fame that unlike virtually every other novelist, his face with its long beard and poufs of hair is quite recognizable—surrounded by a succession of tiny figures representing the characters in his novels.

The painting was never finished, and most of the figures are in black and white, sketched in lightly, ghostly. They have a sort of bothersome swarmlike air to them, as though they are buzzing around his head with the annoying insistence of insects, and perhaps they were, not as fictional figures but as elements of Dickens's past, from which he would have been happy to be free. (And was during much of his lifetime. Only a few intimates knew of Dickens's tortured past, although others could have divined it through the telltale mixture of confidence and self-doubt he carried always with him. In an 1885 book on the history of English literature, for example, the writer is described as merely moving from Portsmouth to London with his family. No blacking factory, no debtors' prison.) No wonder the London of his novels is both a place in which fortune can be found and in which degradation lurks as well. "Midnight had come upon the crowded city," he wrote in *Oliver Twist*. "The palace, the night cellar, the jail, the madhouse— the chambers of birth and death, of health and sickness, the rigid faces of the corpse and the calm sleep of the child—midnight was upon them all."

In Buss's portrait, Dickens sits near a handsome wooden desk with a slant top. It is the same desk that is pictured in an engraving in the Dickens house with the sentimental title "The Empty Chair," an engraving done on the day of Dickens's death in 1870. And the selfsame desk sits in what was the writer's study in the Dickens House Museum, entombed in a glass case like a fragment of the True Cross.

The case bears witness to the other Dickens, the opposite number of the impoverished boy tormented by his father's disgrace. Critics have often found the writer's novels unpersuasive because they tend to divide into two parts, the black hole of poverty, despair, and decay, and an inordinately satisfactory salvation, usually by the good people of the new middle class. (Unlike many English writers, almost no one with a title or an estate turns up in Dickens. The well-to-do tend to be the sort of people that Jane Austen's characters describe as "in trade.") The man himself found this formula persuasive because it had been the story of his life, and its reality must have been as real to him as the enormous and ornate Spanish mahogany sideboard that sits against one wall of the dining room in Doughty Street and which Dickens lugged from one home to another after buying it in 1839. Like Scrooge in *A Christmas Carol,* Dickens was able to leave his past behind.

But his liberation came not through the salvation of spirits but through that most modern mechanism of re-creation: He became a self-made man, then a celebrity, that thing that makes a person simultaneously both more and less than they truly are. This was comparatively rare before the age of mass communications, and rarer still for writers. Rare indeed for writers of any literary merit—by contrast Jane Austen wrote under the pseudonym "A Lady," and Milton's first publisher of *Paradise Lost* was a bookseller who gave the writer five pounds up front and promised another five after 1,300 copies of the first edition were sold.

In his own lifetime, Dickens milked his notoriety for all it was worth in a way recognizable even to today's readers of tabloids and *Hello!* magazine (in the U.K.) or *People* (in the U.S.). Copies of the sheet music for the David Copperfield polka and the Pickwick quadrille are framed and hung on the walls of the Doughty Street house, along with theater programs of plays based upon his work and others in which he appeared. He loved to participate in theatrical productions; he dressed extravagantly and socialized constantly, did reading tours in both England and America at which he was mobbed by fans. He even was pestered by that recognizable celebrity accoutrement, the sycophant relation; Dickens's impecunious father, who had forced him into the blacking factory as a boy with his spending habits, dogged him when he became a public figure. As soon as *Pickwick* became a success, the elder Dickens turned up at his son's publisher, cadging a loan he would never repay.

The Doughty Street house, to which the writer moved his family when only the first of his ten children had been born, was just a way station in his meteoric rise. It was vacated for a larger house just south of Regent's Park, a rich man's house Dickens himself described as "a house of great promise (and great premium), undeniable situation and excessive splendor" with the novelistic address of 1 Devonshire Terrace. That house is gone now, as is his later home, the Gad's Hill Place house in which he died. Dickens's wife Catherine was as fungible as those homes—a starter marriage, perhaps, mirrored in the unsatisfactory relationships with pretty and tractable young women in several of the novels. (David Copperfield, for one, extricates himself from his starter marriage through the fortuitous death of his "child wife," Dora.) Dickens's rise reads as though he was writing the original celebrity primer, minus the drugs: At the height of his fame, he left Catherine for a young actress.

Across the street from the Doughty Street house is another, almost identical building with one of the ubiquitous blue plaques. This one reads "Sydney Smith, 1771–1843, Author and Wit lived here." How extraordinarily depressing it must have been for Sydney Smith, author and wit, as the career of the gangly man across the street inflated like a hot-air balloon until finally the four-story terrace house would no longer hold it: *Pickwick* in 1837, *Oliver Twist* in 1838, *Nicholas Nickleby* in 1839. Even a writer many decades removed is breathless with admiration and envy, especially after reading a visitor's description of an evening at Doughty Street:

"What, you here?" he exclaimed; "I'll bring down my work." It was his monthly portion of "Oliver Twist" for Bentley's. In a few minutes he returned, manuscript in hand, and while he was pleasantly discoursing he employed himself in carrying to the corner of the room a little table, at which he seated himself and recommenced his writing. We, at his bidding, went on talking our "little nothings"— he, every now and then (the feather of his pen still moving rapidly from side to side), put in a cheerful interlude.

Can this be true, writing and entertaining simultaneously? If so, the absence of effort was deceptive. Seeing Dickens's original manuscripts on view in his first house is oddly cheering; they are heavily edited by the author himself, more obscuring loop-the-loops and censorious black cross outs than acceptable prose. I remember the first time I saw the manuscript of *A Christmas Carol*, which is in the Morgan Library in New York City, and realized how hard the man was on himself and how unsatisfactory he found his first drafts. There was that thrill of fellowship; even the greatest of writers can make terrible mistakes.

CHAPTER EIGHT

T urn off Oxford Street, that most generic of London thoroughfares, chockablock with the kind of dime-a-dozen tourist shops you can find in any American and most European cities: cheap luggage emporiums, *bureaus de change,* narrow stores that sell tee shirts and backpacks and the occasional hash pipe. Turn off Oxford Street, since there is really no reason to stay on it, and you will eventually find yourself on Baker Street. The simple utilitarian name produces a faint frisson of excitement, and your step quickens as you read the house numbers. Eventually there it is: 221.

Oh, my. A large office block called Abbey House stands on the spot, with a sign that reads: "Flexible lease available on first floor." Next to it is a small metal plaque, much less handsome or compelling than the literary plaques on other buildings around town, with the bas-relief of a well-known profile. Note to those who have never read the books that detail the exploits of Sherlock Holmes: He didn't actually wear a deerstalker hat. Although his image on the sign does.

Every once in a while a literary location in London is so deeply disappointing that it is scarcely tenable. Dickens's house may be a little overwrought, and unless I read addresses very badly, the rooms in which Lord Peter Wimsey set up housekeeping before he married Harriet Vane are in fact precisely on the site of the Park Lane Hotel, which I suppose is as fitting a fictional bait and switch as you could imagine.

But the Baker Street location is probably the most disappointing in the city. It is not only that the apartments the legendary detective kept at 221b Baker Street, the most famous address in the mystery genre, no longer stand, those rooms presided over by the landlady Mrs. Hudson where, according to Watson, the great man kept "his cigars in the coal scuttle, his tobacco in the toe end of a Persian slipper, and his unanswered correspondence transfixed by a jack knife into the very center of his wooden mantelpiece." (And where the great man also "in one of his queer humors, would sit in an armchair with his hair-trigger and a hundred Boxer cartridges, and proceed to adorn the opposite wall with a patriotic V. R. done in bullet-pocks.")

It is that, tragically, they have been phonied up farther down the street. Somehow, between numbers 237 and 241, in a gerrymander worthy of an old Chicago politician, a 221b has sprung up, complete with a young man in an ill-fitting bobby's uniform outside. (No Lestrade, this, even on his worst days!) The Sherlock Holmes food and beverage and a Sherlock Holmes memorabilia shop stand between the Beatles Store and Elvisly Yours. Across the street is another Holmes store, this one with a variety of mugs, pitchers, and a chess set with, among its pieces, a black dog that is clearly meant to be the menacing Hound of the Baskervilles but looks more like a fat lab, begging.

It's not simply that I find all of this dispiriting, but that Holmes himself, who is as vivid a character as we will find in fiction and who loathed sentiment, much less pretense, would have found it an outrage.

Luckily there are also times and places in which London is vividly, completely that place that you've encountered dozens of times in books. And it's not at the palaces, or staring at diadems in the Tower jewelry exhibition, or even listening to some cabbie do a little mock cockney act because he's come to believe that's the sure way to get stupid Americans to ante up a big tip.

But when you've cut through one of the narrow alleys that leads from Green Park to Pall Mall, skirting the majestically restored Spencer House, wandering out onto St. James's Street, it's rather clear that you're not in Kansas, or even Manhattan, anymore. The shopwindow of Williams Evans, "gun and rifle makers," is filled with hunting paraphernalia of the most tasteful and arcane sort, shooting coats and moleskin plus 2s and the House Tweed laird's jacket. Just up the street, a store with a beautiful assortment of top hats and bonnets trimmed with feathers and ribbons has a sign displayed near the front door: "Now Taking Orders For Ascot."

Up on Piccadilly, the shopping arcades are as Victorian as anyone could want, with their ivory-handled shaving brushes and handmade boots. The one between Albemarle and Bond Streets is particularly atmospheric, with its enormous bay windows and gilded signs. Queen Victoria bought her riding habits in one of the shops, and it looks and feels as if the servant sent on the task had only lately left.

But perhaps it is in Simpson's-in-the-Strand that I felt most definitely ensconced in the London I'd learned to love through books, a stage-set London that is only a highly colored, largely antiquated facsimile of the real thing. That feeling may have been inevitable, since English food plays such a central part in how Americans see England, and also how they see it in a way that is painfully out-of-date. It exists, as does so much else in English novels, in a completely foreign argot: even such a thing as tea, which we assume to be a simple beverage, turns out upon further reading to be something more, and more mysterious, perhaps with cakes, perhaps with cucumber sandwiches, perhaps with some mysterious element called clotted cream or mysterious side dish called digestive biscuits. And that is quite apart from completely foreign dishes like toad-in-the-hole or bangers and mash.

An acquaintance of mine once wrote a cookbook entitled *Great English Food,* and she said that not a single person to whom she had given it or spoken of it in the United States could keep a straight face, and some actually believed that the entire book was a joke. But it was in fact filled with the sort of food that is served at Simpson's-in-the-Strand, and was served there before any current Londoner was actually alive. (Although by London standards it is considered quite a baby; Simpson's was founded in the early nineteenth century.) You know what you're going to get when you enter its dining room, called the Grand Divan, which features paneling as dark and glossy and plaster ceilings as richly ornamented as those in a Victorian novel of the upper classes. And if you didn't apprehend the menu from your surroundings, you can intuit it from the 1910 novel *Howards End,* in which the heroine has "humourously lamented" that she has never been there—even then, it was a bit of an old fogy spot—and is taken to lunch by the older man she will later marry. "What'll you have?" he asks.

"Fish pie," said she, with a glance at the menu.

"Fish pie! Fancy coming for fish pie to Simpson's. It's not a bit the thing to go for here."

And finally he concludes, "Saddle of mutton, and cider to drink. That's the type of thing. I like this place, for a joke, once in a way. It is so thoroughly Old English."

And it still is. Most of the wait staff spends the lunch hours pushing around silver-domed trolleys under which are enormous joints of meat and side portions of Yorkshire pudding. It is also possible to order potted shrimps, steak-and-kidney pudding, treacle sponge, and a savoury of Welsh rarebit—in short, an English meal impervious to the passage of time or culinary fashion. Very little on the menu would be available, or even desirable, in any New York City restaurant I know. "It's a pity, really," said one of my London book editors.

"At lunch in New York no one eats, no one smokes, and no one drinks."

That about covers it.

Most of my London acquaintances were quick to remind me that Simpson's, although it has long had a reputation for literary lunches, was now serving them mostly to editors preparing to retire to a cottage in the Cotswolds, and that there were plenty of restaurants in Notting Hill or even around the Inns of Court that served rare tuna and mesclun salads to the younger, hipper set. But I reminded them right back that it is often at the flagrant margins that we learn to first attach ourselves to a place. That's why many of us who become Anglophiles in absentia, as it were, did so originally not through great literature, Defoe or Dr. Johnson, but through mystery stories and romantic novels, through manservants like Bunter and Lugg and heroes who gambled at Boodles and bought their boots in Bond Street.

For many Americans of a certain age, that Technicolor London first presented itself in the form of a big book about the glories of the city written by a woman who had never actually been there. *Forever Amber* was published in 1944, when the war had made satins and velvets an impossible luxury and the real world a sad, gray, and tattered place. It sold 100,000 copies in its first week and was the bestselling book in the United States during the decade after its publication. This despite—or perhaps because of—the widespread denunciations of the novel by religious and civic leaders as obscene and immoral, a denunciation that seems quaint in light of today's standards for sex scenes and language.

Nominally, *Forever Amber* is a story set during the Restoration about a courtesan with the overwrought name of Amber St. Clare. Charles II is an important character, and so are a number of actual nobleman from his court. Amber is not only impregnated by the king and imprisoned in Newgate (like her more moral, more realistic fictional sister Moll Flanders); she also survives both the Great Plague and the Great Fire of London.

Like most bodice rippers, *Forever Amber* may smell of sex, but it's really about love, the undying love Amber feels, even while married to a succession of husbands and entertaining a succession of lovers, for a buff guy named Bruce, or, as she likes to call him, "Lord Carlton." It's also about a great love affair with a great city, the city of London. Unlike the denizens of London described by Dickens, who are trapped in its narrow and filthy streets as surely as if they were behind prison walls, or those of Evelyn Waugh, who unthinkingly pass through town on their way to one social event or another, the heroine of Kathleen Winsor's novel is beside herself with emotion whenever she considers her adopted home. "Oh, London, London, I love you," she cries on her first day there. And that's on page fifty-three of a nearly thousand-page novel.

And the London she describes is a place worthy of that love, and still visible in spots today. There's a nice description of Amber riding out of town to snare an unsuspecting dupe in the village of Knightsbridge. While Knightsbridge is now as much a part of the main body of London as London Bridge, it is possible to walk through its side streets and small squares and understand how the great swathe of green designated for hunting by the king, later to become Green Park—not to mention the torturous horseback travel of the day—would have relegated it to village status. Amber takes up lodgings at a house called The Plume of Feathers: "A large wooden sign swung out over the street just below Amber's parlour windows—it depicted a great swirling blue plume painted on a gilt background, and was supported by a very ornate wrought-iron frame, also gilded." Of course, any London visitor can see a similar sign hanging from any one of a dozen pubs. And the shops where Amber is seen with Bruce by his wife sound remarkably like the shopping arcades—odd, because the action of the novel takes place years before those arcades were built.

Or not so odd, perhaps. While I was on a trip to London, the author of *Forever Amber*, Kathleen Winsor, died at the age of eighty-three, and in a lively obituary in the *Guardian* a writer described her book thus: "It was a love letter to a London she had read about in Defoe and Pepys, but had never seen." He went on to describe how the twenty-four-year-old American had been inspired by her husband's thesis on Charles II and had written her spectacular maiden success with the help of years of research and an enormous map of Restoration London. How odd it was to know that one of the writers who had first taught me to love London—because, given all the talk about how dirty *Amber* was, it was a must-read for teenage girls even twenty years after its publication—was also a writer who had fallen for the city at a distance, created it in her mind's eye, as well as on the page.

CHAPTER NINE

L uckily on that visit to London I had a more historically accurate opportunity to visit its rich past.
The British Museum had just opened a show on London
1753, as though someone had known I was coming and
would only be able to stomach so much of Internet cafés
and Starbucks lattes and all the one-world paraphernalia that has so homogenized foreign travel. The British
Museum is not crowded in on the Brompton Road with
the Victoria and Albert, the Natural History, and the
Science Museums. Nor is it one of the gems in the neck-
lace of important places that curves around Trafalgar
Square: the National Gallery and the National Portrait

Gallery with their columns and plinths and plumes of water trumpeting their importance.

The British Museum is instead surrounded by bookstores and other small shops and houses in the midst of Bloomsbury, in such an unlikely setting that one shopkeeper a block away said that when he saw people enter with cameras and guidebooks he knew instantly to say, "Left at the end of the street, then down and it's on the right hand" even before they'd opened their mouths. Perhaps as well as any other great London institution the museum plays with the idea of how past and present conjoin. The building itself does the trick, by combining a square and stodgy classical Greek temple facade with a glass-and-steel skylit roof over the great court. The transparent roof went in in 2000 and is an absolutely magical marriage of technology, beauty, and function. (Contrary to Gershwin's "Foggy Day" lament, the British Museum has not lost its charm.) And inside the museum itself, for those of us who tend to think of the London Wall as venerable antiquity, there is the Rosetta stone and the famous mummies, as well as Greek, Asian, and Mexican treasures procured for the museum by generations of distinguished archaeological grave robbers.

So while the London show spoke to my inner antiquarian, its material was, in fact, by the British

Museum's standards, rather recent. The wonderful thing about it, however, was that it did what London, in its history and its variety, has always done—it showed clearly that there is really nothing new under the sun.

That, I think, is one of the most valuable lessons I've learned from reading English literature, the kind of unvarying nature both of social problems and personal dramas. There is very little to separate, say, Georgette Heyer's Regency drama *Arabella,* about a young woman muddling through her long-awaited London season, from Nancy Mitford's Radlett girls in *The Pursuit of Love,* except for the passage of time and the claims of craft. Dances, dresses, men, marriage. The hypochondriacal moneylender Mrs. Islam in Monica Ali's contemporary novel *Brick Lane* may be a Bangladeshi immigrant, but she is also a Dickens character in a modern London setting. John Mortimer's hapless Rumpole, married to She Who Must Be Obeyed and drinking cheap plonk after representing yet another of the Timsons—"A family to breed from, the Timsons. Must almost keep the old Bailey going singlehanded"—owes a bit to Chaucer, a bit to Waugh. And all of the above owe more than a bit to real life; their like can be found in the London papers on any given day, being charged with usury, being indicted for fraud, representing those so indicted.

Most of those peering at the Hogarth engravings and Canaletto paintings in the 1753 show on its first day were aged, and so were the stories the exhibits told. Yet they were also the stories we tell ourselves every day now, to convince ourselves that the golden age is past: raging crime, class warfare, invasive immigrants, light morals, public misbehavior. Always we convince ourselves that the parade of unwelcome and despised is a new phenomenon, which is why the phrase "the good old days" has passed from cliché into self-parody. Joseph Conrad, a Polish émigré writing in English, saw this with the harshest of eyes in *The Secret Agent:* "a peculiarly London sun" is "at a moderate elevation about Hyde Park Corner with an air of punctual and benign vigilance," and the man walking beneath it considers the gap between rich and poor, in the fashion of Conrad's highly political novels, and how "the whole social order favourable to their hygienic idleness had to be protected against the shallow enviousness of unhygienic labour."

There's no getting away from the fact that the 1753 exhibit is full of echoes of a more modern London, as well as reflections of an older, perhaps even harsher city. Hogarth's rendering of "A View of Cheapside, as it appeared on Lord Mayor's Day Last," looks fairly similar to Piccadilly Circus on any given Saturday night, except for the Lord Mayor's coach and the presence of the King and Queen watching from an awninged balcony. The crush at the scene is a testimonial to what was happening then and what is happening again today: That is, that those with money and standing, who in the past had largely lived in the country and visited town only on shopping trips and special occasions, had decided instead that it was important to have a place in London. "To a lover of books the shops and sales in London present irresistible temptations," wrote Edward Gibbon, who sold his father's country estate, acquired a lapdog and a parrot, and rented a flat in Cavendish Square, where he wrote *The Decline and Fall of the Roman Empire.*

There was also, according to the exhibit's companion guide, the requisite hostility toward immigrants. They were simply different immigrants than today's Brick Lane Bangladeshis or Brixton Jamaicans. Scots, Jews, Irish, French Huguenots. There was, in the opinion of many native Londoners, something wrong with each of them, and they were certain to lower the tone and sully the streets. Many of them set up shop, but not on Bond Street, where the quality shopped, then as now.

Talk of farthingales and arsenic powder makes us also assume that fashions in dress were completely unlike our own, and indeed the tight trousers and slashed skirts of Soho would shock and amaze any of the ladies of 1753 London. But in the British Museum exhibit, there are a pair of women's shoes as pretty as any in a Notting Hill boutique now, blue-green silk encrusted with silver lace, with a small curved heel, and alongside the shoes are some bejeweled hair ornaments, gold and silver with garnets. You could sell either in a sec in Harvey Nick's to one of those girls in tight trousers.

White's and Boodles in Mayfair were the best clubs then, not the more bohemian hangouts of modern London, the Soho and the Groucho, where, one account has it, the artist Damien Hirst was banned for being too casual about exposing himself. (Of course, literature would create its own clubs, some even more compelling. Sherlock Holmes's brother Mycroft is a member of the Diogenes Club on Pall Mall, a club in which "no member is permitted to take the least notice of any other one." And Adam Dalgliesh, the poet who is also P. D. James's Scotland Yard superintendent, occasionally dines at the Cadaver Club on Tavistock Square, whose members are men "with an interest in murder.")

For the working man of 1753, one great pleasure was the coffeehouse. There were hundreds of them, all doing a booming business, although to listen to people inveigh against the proliferation of Nero's decaf take-away latte and the like, you would swear they were purely a modern invention. In the coffeehouses were the newspapers: "All Englishmen are great newsmongers," one French observer wrote.

Which brings us to the case of Elizabeth Canning. While the London tabloids of our own time were mining the cases of two women accused of infanticide and another who had killed two young boys when she herself was a child, Elizabeth's case was the tabloid equivalent of three centuries ago, her bad press now encased in glass exhibition cases. The eighteen-year-old scullery maid disappeared on New Year's Day, 1753, and when she turned up again a month later she said she'd been kidnapped. Two old women were arrested for the crime, and both found guilty: One was branded on the thumb and sentenced to the notorious Newgate prison—"black as a Newgate knocker," they once said of the lock of hair thieves wore behind one ear—and the other, incredibly, sentenced to death because she had allegedly stolen Elizabeth's stays, worth about ten shillings.

When an alibi surfaced for one woman and a judge became suspicious of Canning's claims, the alleged stealer of the stays, a woman named Mary Squires (always described in the press as "the old gypsy") was pardoned by the king. Broadsides showed plans of the house where Canning was allegedly held, which she was apparently unable to describe accurately although it consisted of little more than two small downstairs rooms and an attic. Her portrait appeared in the papers in profile, in a cap and short cape. Another popular illustration showed Canning, who was herself tried for perjury, in the dock; the publisher exercised a master stroke of economy and, instead of using a new drawing, merely recycled the copperplate of the trial of a highwayman named James Maclaine, erasing Maclaine and having an artist draw the figure of a young woman in his place.

All of London divided into pro- and anti-Canning camps. Some gossiped that she had disappeared to hide a pregnancy and birth; others collected hundreds of pounds for her and invited her to be feted at the fashionable White's in St. James's. Her story could be transplanted wholesale into today's papers or infotainment news shows, except for her eventual punishment: She was exiled to America. Perhaps, like John Lennon, Tina Brown, and a clutch of other famous British subjects, she went on to find happiness there. Or perhaps it was a true execution by inches, as the Anglophile Henry James would have it. Near the end of *The*

Henry James, 1843-1916

Portrait of A Lady, there is an exchange between Isabel and Mrs. Touchett that makes the novelist's position clear: "Do you still like Serena Merle?" the older woman asks our heroine.

"Not as I once did. But it doesn't matter, for she's going to America."

"To America? She must have done something very bad."

"Yes—very bad."

CHAPTER TEN

Envy is a writer's lot in London, and not only because so many great writers have walked its streets. (And continue to do so—during my first stay at the Groucho Club, I glimpsed Salman Rushdie drinking at the bar. This seemed notable mainly because it was at the height of the very public *fatwa* against him by conservative Muslim clerics, who had threatened death in return for the purported blasphemy of his novel *The Satanic Verses.* It was said that Rushdie was in hiding. The bar at the Groucho was quite dark, so perhaps it was as good a place as any to hide.)

There simply could not be a better place in which to set a story. After the Great Fire destroyed so much of the city, Christopher Wren proposed that it should be re-created along a more sensible grid system. This would have made London immeasurably easier to negotiate—when a stranger is lost in London, she is lost indeed—and sensible in a way that it is not now and never has been. Thank God the proposal was considered, and rejected. The city that rose from the ashes rose along the same nonsensical system of country lanes and downhill passages that had defined it before. And so it reasserted itself as a kind of mazelike mystery that is irresistible for the imaginative mind.

It is, perhaps, Dickens who best describes the allure of the architecture when he speaks of Scrooge's rooms in "a lowering pile of building up a yard, where it had so little business to be, that one could scarcely help fancying it must have run there when it was a young house, playing at hide and seek with other houses, and forgotten the way out again." There are countless buildings that seem trapped in the narrow backstreets of the West End or Chelsea, streets designed for one century and trying to make do in another. At Piccadilly there is a warning sign that Jermyn Street, home of the the shirtmakers Turnbull and Asser and the perfumier Floris, is "unsuited for long vehicles."

For someone used to the tidy, slightly boring numbered streets of upper Manhattan, it is a joy to encounter St. James's Street, St. James's Place and Little St. James's Street. Every street name seems to have a codicil attached, a cartographic family tree; as Thackeray noted, "All the world knows that Lord Steyne's town palace stands in Gaunt Square, out of which Great Gaunt Street leads." Nearby, according to the novelist, is New Gaunt Street, and Gaunt Mews. All this would seem like satire if you did not see it all around you in the city itself.

So a lover of language finds herself enamored of geography here. The placenames alone are a gift to a novelist. If there is anywhere in the world that sounds grander than Belgravia, I'd like to know it; Fifth Avenue, by comparison, is just a number. Elephant and Castle, Camberwell, Stepney, Bethnal Green. Bolingbroke Grove, Threadneedle Street, Cadogan Terrace, Lavender Sweep, Leadenhall Market, Half Moon Street, Queen's Circus, Queen's Club Gardens, Queen's Gate Mews. The *London A to Z* is a tone poem that could easily be arranged as blank verse of a high order. In fact, the Scottish mystery novelist Anne Perry has cribbed from it unashamedly, naming her novels after London locales in which they are set, Southampton Road, Rutland Place, Cardington Crescent, and the like. (London does not rename things; while America is now rife with John F. Kennedy Boulevards, there is no Churchill Street or Princess Diana Avenue.)

Meanwhile the American mystery writer Martha Grimes has chosen to name her books after pubs, a decision that is so sensible, given the richness and variety of public house names, that the only wonder is that it wasn't done years before. In just a week in London, a tourist making a haphazard list comes up with the Shakespeare, the Samuel Pepys, the Bag O'Nails, the Dog and Duck, the Friend at Hand, the Porcupine, and the Coal Hole. In his magnificent book, *London: A Biography,* the novelist Peter Ackroyd writes that in 1854 there were seventy King's Heads, ninety King's Arms, seventy Crowns, fifty Queen's Heads, thirty Foxes, and thirty Swans. There were some twenty thousand pubs to chose from in all at the time.

(One Friday evening, wandering through Shepherd Market, we came upon a crush of people in one of the narrow cobbled back alleys laughing and chatting and holding glasses in front of a cattycornered establishment called Ye Grapes and concluded that we were intruding on an office party or some other kind of official gathering. "Probably just an evening out at the local," said a friend, quite correctly, as it turned out. Reading about public drinking and drunkenness, especially the liberal use of gin, is an essential part of knowing London through books. It turns out that that, too, has changed little, even in a more abstemious time.)

The *A to Z* was assembled originally by a woman who walked nearly twenty miles a day and covered three thousand miles of streets. Perhaps at the end she felt as if she truly knew London. If so, she might be alone in that. "London is a labyrinth, half of stone and half of flesh," writes Ackroyd in his introduction. "It cannot be conceived in its entirety but can be experienced only as a wilderness of alleys and passages, courts and thoroughfares, in which even the most experienced citizen may lose the way." Ackroyd's book, in my worn and spotted paperback edition, is more than eight hundred pages. After walking the streets of London, it does not seem excessive.

And his point about experiencing the city episodically may be the key to why it is such a spectacular starting point for fiction; the episode is, after all, how we novelists do what we do. Virginia Woolf once said in a letter to her sister, "To write a novel in the heart of London is next to an impossibility. I feel as if I were nailing a flag to the top of a mast in a raging gale." But that's nonsense, made more nonsensical by how many wonderful things the writer managed to produce while in the midst of the storm of the city. In fact it may be exactly the opposite: The small and quiet spot offers so much less, so many fewer of the telling details that are so critical to a sense of place. These are the details that are right there for the observing in a city so diverse, so polyglot, so hodgepodge.

In a sweetly elegiac memoir entitled *Winter in London* published more than a half century ago, a writer named Ivor Brown wrote quite correctly, "Great men have lifted their fictions from these pavements; the ghosts of any London lane are infinite." It is impossible not to feel them peeking over your shoulder and, if so inclined, to find inspiration in their generations. To sink down on a bench with the inscription "From members of hall in memory of the first Earl of Birkenhead" on one of the paths that crisscross Gray's Inn must speak to even the uninspired. If nothing else it is a perfect aesthetic moment, a balance in absolute equipoise of muted red brick, bright green grass, gravel, and window glass glinting in the sunlight. Trollope captured the atmosphere perfectly and simply in one of his Palliser novels, *The Prime Minister,* when he described the offices of Mr. Wharton: "He had a large pleasant room in which to sit, looking out from the ground floor of Stone Buildings on to the gardens belonging to the Inn—and here, in the center of the metropolis, but in perfect quiet as far as the outside world was concerned, he had lived and still lived his life." The gardens were planted by Francis Bacon. The first performance of Comedy of Errors was in the hall. The ghosts are most distinguished.

Or, if you are of a mind to write something more florid and romantic, there is always the Albert Memorial, which all by itself must explode forever the notion of the English as an emotionally distant race. Down the Broad Walk or across the Flower Walk in Kensington Gardens, and suddenly, there it is, like a great bejeweled costume brooch in a case of enameled Asprey cufflinks.

It is a poem, or a short story, or perhaps a comic book all by itself, and a shock to the system: statues and carvings representing the continents and commerce, engineering, agriculture, and manufacturing, yards of gilded fencing, and at the center a vast altarpiece of elaborate mosaics, atop it, not a tabernacle, but "Albert," as it says on the base, as though there had been no other before or since. He is more than twice life-size, including his famous muttonchop whiskers, and blindingly gold.

Albert Memorial, Kensington Gardens

During the war the statue was darkened so that enemy planes would not use it as a marker to attack Kensington Palace, but a thousand books of gold leaf used in a recent renovation brought Albert back to where he was meant to be: as good an evocation of deranged adoration as exists outside the leap of a widow onto a ceremonial pyre. Victoria built the monument in memory of her beloved prince; just across the road is the Royal Albert Hall, which was meant to be called the Hall of Arts and Sciences. The widowed Queen shocked everyone when she laid the cornerstone, christened the building, and unexpectedly added the late consort's name. The shock seems overdone; if the bystanders had only looked across the street at the blinding rococo of the Albert Memorial, they might have wondered when the Queen would rechristen St. Paul's Cathedral and the British Museum in Albert's name as well!

Of course it is not only the great monuments that make the London scene rich in inspiration, but the small corners and commonplaces as well. Eaton Square, all abloom between solemn white-columned rows of houses, still bespeaks privilege and a dignified self-possession, that thing the Mitford sisters mocked as U, for Upper class. But it's for sure people of wealth and accomplishment once thought of as arrivistes are ensconced within some of its homes now. (After all, an Egyptian who can't get himself British citizenship owns Harrods, and has complemented its almost medieval food court, with its eels and rabbits and quail, with an ill-advised Egyptian hall!) The taxi drivers' houses scattered around the city, where cabbies can have a cup of tea and a chat (or a grouse) still remain, even if some of the cabbies are Indian or Jamaican. And on Vigo Street a man in full old-fashioned London regalia—balmacaan, waistcoat, suit, tie, and umbrella by his side—sells orchids from a stall. What in the world can his story be? Perhaps I'll just invent it.

Then again, maybe not. It's the ghosts that might be inclined to keep writers away from London as well as to draw them. If the sight of full bookshelves sometimes make us wonder whether another book is really the answer to any question, then the streets of London respond resoundingly. No more about Pall Mall! No more about St. James's! No more about the highhanded doorman or the beggar with his dog. (Is it affirming or dispiriting, to read in Peter Ackroyd's book on London that historically the dog "has always been the companion of the London outcast," the beggar's "only companion in this world of need," then to walk out to Piccadilly and find a homeless man, with a sand-colored mixed breed, in front of the Pret A Manger

sandwich shop with a sign "My Dog Needs Food.")
Being a writer is a continually humbling experience,
carrying within it always rejection, by editors and
readers, the cognoscenti, and the marketplace. The
books of London suggest a deeper, more punishing
rejection: the rejection of surfeit. The deed was done
long ago, and brilliantly. Being a writer living in
London must be like being a chef in Paris, or a priest
in Rome—intimidating, and with good reason. V. S.
Pritchett once wrote, " London has the effect of making one feel personally historic." But his writing has
always given me the impression that Pritchett tends to
feel personally historic a great deal. For an American
writer, London can have the effect of making you feel
personally insignificant.

Even writing about London itself brings you
smack up against it, against Henry Fielding and
Boswell, or fellow Americans like Mark Twain or the
anglophile Henry James. Virginia Woolf, sadly, has
now become known to modern Americans chiefly as
Nicole Kidman in a prosthetic nose; in her own time
her novel *Mrs. Dalloway,* whose kinesthetic approach
to the whole world all in one day inspired Michael
Cunningham's *The Hours* (and from there the movie
in which Kidman appeared) received a chilly recep-
tion. Members of her own circle were puzzled by it,

and the critic Arnold Bennet wrote, "I could not finish it." But it is not simply that it was one of the first forays into a new, more realistic kind of novel writing—"The method of writing smooth narrative can't be right," Woolf wrote in her diary. "Things don't happen in one's mind like that"—but that it is as good an account of how we experience a beloved place as any in literature. During the course of her errands, Clarissa Dalloway ecstatically breathes in the palpable London around her in the way we all have done when we are in the midst of a place we know and treasure, whether it be the country, the town, or the city. In the process she takes one of London's most predictable and therefore almost invisible icons and makes it new again:

> For having lived in Westminster—
> how many years now? over twenty,—one
> feels even in the midst of traffic or wak-
> ing at night, Clarissa was positive, a
> particular hush, or solemnity; an inde-
> scribable pause; a suspense (but that
> might be her heart, affected, they said,
> by influenza) before Big Ben strikes.
> There! Out it boomed. First a warning,
> musical; then the hour, irrevocable.

The leaden circles dissolved in the air. Such fools we are, she thought, crossing Victoria Street. For Heaven only knows why one loves it so, how one sees it so, making it up, building it round one, tumbling it, creating it every moment afresh; but the veriest frumps, the most dejected of miseries sitting on doorsteps (drink their downfall) do the same; can't be dealt with, she felt positive, by Acts of Parliament for that very reason: they love life. In people's eyes, in the swing, tramp and trudge; in the bellow and the uproar; the carriages, motor cars, omnibuses, vans, sandwich men shuffling and swinging; brass bands; barrel organs; in the triumph and the jingle and the strange high singing of some aeroplane overhead was what she loved; life; London; this moment in June.

That's a good bit to quote in your own work from someone else's, but it so vividly illustrates the point that London makes: that it has been known, and known by experts. (And another point, too, not confined to

London; Lytton Strachey may not have thought well of *Mrs. Dalloway,* but like many brilliant British critics throughout the course of human existence, he was full of it.) This is a great gift to resident and visitor alike, but it is tough on those of us who search for fresh and individual ways to describe it. But the attempt must be made, the pilgrimage taken. What are all those small, oval, enameled plaques but a goad to the daunted spirit, a flag with the legend "It can be done!" By H. G. Wells and Elizabeth Bowen, by John Keats and Somerset Maugham. There are more than seven hundred of the plaques, and that, too, carries a double message: so much has been said, but many voices can be heard.

That is why, on my latest trip to the city, I came with my eldest child, my writer son. A bit of background psychological, not geographic: It became clear to me that Sigmund Freud was on to something with his Oedipal theory several years ago, when the boy began to become a man. Part of his passage into adulthood, I understood, was to separate from me convincingly through a prolonged period of covert removal and outright rejection. I suspected this was bad for him; I knew for a fact that it was bad for me. So I determined that I was going to transmute our relationship slowly from one of mother and son to one of writer and writer.

Take that, Dr. Freud.

(There is, by the by, a Freud museum in North London, in the house where he lived after fleeing Vienna once the Nazis came goosestepping in. It contains the master's original couch, as well as a Freud gift shop. I have never been there, perhaps because it is more entertaining to imagine the gift shop in my mind's eye, perhaps because the whole theory of penis envy still makes me, to use a persistent literary Englishism, quite cross.)

The ruse worked, and never more splendidly than when I brought my son, then nineteen, to act as another set of eyes, ears, and constantly moving feet while I considered imaginary London. But it was not simply to persuade him of the brilliance of Dickens or the wit of Thackeray or the art of Woolf that I brought him, or set him to work rummaging through my old books for passages that spoke to him. ("Can you remember why you marked this?" he said to me once about a line in Yeats, a moment when we agreed to disagree about our tastes and writerly inclinations.) It was to hand down the possibility without the fear, the greatness without the intimidation. And the legacy. Herewith the world of Chaucer and Browning, T. S. Eliot and Graham Greene. You are a writer; you are welcome here.

"Are you intimidated by London?" I asked.

"Why?" he said.

Youth may be wasted on the young, as George Bernard Shaw once said, but not always.

CHAPTER ELEVEN

I t's ironic that much of this literary pedigree began in what is now one of London's least atmospheric areas. Southwark certainly has more cachet now than it had only a few decades ago, but it is the luster of its resurrection, not of its long rich history. The name reflects its location; it's that big bump on the map south of the Thames that seems to push the river closer to the Strand and the Tower and all those better-known places that lie on the north side. There used to be a standing joke that to go to Southwark you needed a visa, in the same way Manhattanites like to joke about the other four boroughs of New York City.

Yet its literary pedigree is greater than that of Bloomsbury or the Inns of Court or any of the other London neighborhoods that have housed writers and their imagined characters. Because it was long ago the last great stopping-off place before London Bridge, then chockablock with houses all its length, it was a kind of frontier London, just beyond the reach of its laws and its social mores, a welter of taverns, gambling houses, and various other dens of iniquity. The pilgrims in *The Canterbury Tales* start their journey "in Southwerk at the Tabard." Shakespeare's Globe was there, and it's said he lived in Southwark when he did some of his best work. Samuel Pepys apparently watched the Great Fire of London from a tavern on the Bankside.

And in Lant Street in Southwark, the young Dickens took up residence while the rest of his family was nearby in the Marshalsea, the long-gone debtors' prison in which whole families lived, some with drapes and sideboards and pewter plate, until their debts could be settled. More than Doughty Street the area pays tribute to the master: Leigh Hunt Street and Weller Street are named for Pickwickians, and Little Dorrit Church is not far away.

Those rich, often criminal days on the South Bank slipped away. Twenty years after the Great Fire to the north there was another that devastated Southwark.

Little Dorrit Church, Southwark

Many of its old buildings were pulled down in attempts at what we now call urban renewal, and the German bombers turned much of that to rubble. For many years it was a ruin, the part of London that, despite its extraordinary history, tourists never went to see.

Now it is one of the areas that draw them most consistently, although for someone seeking the atmospherics of old London, venerable London, imagined London, it is a little tough to take. Southwark is new London with a vengeance, although a few of its pleasures echo the old, albeit in a perilously self-conscious way. Across the Hungerford footbridge you go, now held aloft by a web of white wires that suggest a spiderweb, to a London whose first face is not narrow lanes and crooked streets but a great open plaza facing the water. Down its length are ranged the sort of people that were once its denizens and were called "buskers." There are musicians, magicians, a man enacting a silent show of marionettes to the music of (yikes!) "A Foggy Day in London Town," and a woman chalking "The Birth of Venus" onto the cement with her empty artists' pastels box by her heel for donations. Days later, on the other side of the river near Tower Bridge, we will see yet another chalk artist copying the same masterpiece. What is it about Botticelli and city pavement?

All this, however, takes place against a backdrop the former occupants of the place, even the most gifted fantabulists, could scarcely have imagined. There is a swathe of grass full of picnickers and young families on blankets, and then a wall of large featureless buildings of no particular modern design around the kind of barren open urban plazas that have turned out to be a mecca for skateboarders. Although Prince Charles seems to have no eye for even distinguished modern architecture, perhaps the inevitable effect of living in a series of eighteenth- and nineteenth- century palaces, he wasn't far off when he said the Royal National Theater building looked like "a disused power station." What's worse, the Tate Modern Museum *is* a disused power station, the Bankside Power Station, decommissioned in 1986, reborn with works by Picasso, Jackson Pollock, and Andy Warhol. Thank God for Southwark Cathedral, with its stained-glass windows showing scenes from Shakespeare, and the reproduction of the Globe Theatre, which was built in the old fashion, with pegs instead of nails. Wandering behind Waterloo Station with its new Janus face, half a staid turn-of-the-twentieth-century block, the other half all cables and glass, there is actual life: several blocks of identical houses, two up, two down, but betraying with their enameled doors, their window treatments, and their window boxes the unmistakable odor of recent gentrification.

It would be easy to be snide about this, particularly in light of the beautiful state of preservation of the north side of the Thames, except for the lessons of history. One is that the original Southwark neighborhoods were the kinds of places residents were tempted to bulldoze, not preserve. The area had been a place for the unwelcome and the unlawful, at one time home to seven prisons, among them the original Clink that gave the name to all the others. It was also one of those areas, common to all great cities, where the undesirable but essential were located, the noxious factories, the tanneries, the soapmakers. Prostitutes worked the streets, radicals hid in the cellars. It was as though the whole area was a place of incarceration where the rest of London sent its troubles to be contained, and when its buildings were torn or closed down, for many who had lived or worked there it was as Dickens had written of the Marshalsea, once part of the area: "The world is none the worse without it."

But it's a mistake for a visitor, particularly one from America, to be disdainful of any London neighborhood where the newly built has taken the place of what went before. We Americans have an inferiority complex about the British, if for no other reason than that the history they carry is so much longer and richer than our own; after all, what passes for a very old building in Boston or Baltimore is merely middle-aged in London. (And we are convinced that British actors are better than our own, simply because their accents are so mellifluous.) But even those who have the usual American inch-deep knowledge of history understand that the small island nation from which we sprang has seen hardship that we cannot compete with. Fires that destroyed entire neighborhoods. Epidemics that wiped out hundreds of thousands of people. The slate of London had already been wiped almost clean many times before America was more than a vast expanse of forest traversed by Indian tribes.

But the city's trials are not simply ancient ones. Perhaps it is the most recent one of which we are most aware, and which we feel most deeply without having felt it personally at all, at least on our home ground. Sometimes you come upon it suddenly, in a way that shocks you into silence. On the Exhibition Row side of the Victoria and Albert Museum is a long wall that parallels the sidewalk. It is pocked with large holes, as though it had at one time been made of softer stuff and someone had thrown one hardball at it after another. Chiseled in among the pockmarks are these words: "The damage to these walls is the result of enemy bombing during the blitz of the second world war 1939–1945 and is left as a memorial to the enduring values of this great museum in a time of conflict."

In some ways it's the literature of the Blitz that makes London feel foreign as much as any Regency romance about carriage rides on Rotten Row and dances at Almack's. Perhaps that's because the stories are simultaneously of our times and yet quite foreign, at least for those who spent those years in America, its buildings pocked only with war bond posters and gold stars. Peter Ackroyd makes it quite vivid at the very end of his London book, very vivid and very humbling. Six hundred bombers dropped their payloads on East London one night in September 1940, then the next night, and the next, hitting St. Paul's Cathedral and Piccadilly. They damaged Buckingham Palace, too, leading the Queen, later the Queen Mother, to famously say that she was glad she'd been bombed because now she could look the East End in the face.

By November, 1940, more than thirty thousand bombs had been dropped on London. Finally at the end of December came the raid that was the culmination of all that had gone before. The City, which was once the center of London and is now the center of finance and of publishing, was attacked. Whole blocks burned to the ground; many churches were severely damaged. Paternoster Row, that address familiar to anyone with

Hospital destroyed in the Blitz, 1940

old English books as the home of book publishing, was entirely destroyed, and, along with it, according to Ackroyd's account, five million books. The offices of dozens of publishers vanished in one night, just as they had during the Great Fire of London.

Some of the best known novels of the time capture this, but in small intimate bits, perhaps in part because this tells the story of ordinary Londoners better than panoramic scenes of destruction would, perhaps because many of the novels of the Blitz were written by women. Nancy Mitford's *The Pursuit of Love* ends amid the strange juxtaposition of bombing raids and daily domestic life. Its narrator, Fanny, married and living in the country, goes up to London. "There had been a heavy raid the night before, and I passed through streets which glistened with broken glass," she says. "Many fires still smoldered, and fire engines, ambulances and rescue men hurried to and fro." But she also captures the almost gleeful pleasure some Londoners took in getting through the disasters, what Ackroyd describes as pride in their own suffering. A cab driver tells Fanny of helping the rescue workers with "a spongy mass of red," adding, "it was still breathing, so I takes it to the hospital, but they says that's no good to us, take it to the mortuary. So I sews it in a sack and takes it to the mortuary."

"Oh, that's nothing to what I have seen," he adds.

"The people now, they don't know what real trouble is," said a talkative cab driver who'd been a child during that time, sent out to the country after the earliest bombs fell.

Elizabeth Bowen's novel *The Heat of the Day* is set entirely during the period, and what it captures is a city deadened by waiting for the worst, going about its business in an atmosphere of banked fear and fire, the "lightless middle of the tunnel." It is not so much the raids she describes as the life around and after them: "And it was now, when you no longer saw, heard, smelled war, that a deadening acclimatization to it began to set in. The first generation of ruins, cleaned up, shored up, began to weather—in daylight they took their places as a norm of the scene." I remember reading this as a teenager and, unaccustomed to any tragedy or deprivation, concluding that Bowen was dull and a little downbeat. Yet she must have made a more powerful impact on my unconscious mind than that conclusion would suggest, since, living in New York on September 11, 2001, I found myself reaching for my old hardcover copy of *The Heat of the Day* and revisiting the story of Stella and Robert's love affair more for that sense of watchful waiting in the face of sudden disaster than anything else.

And Doris Lessing, too, for her sense of what came after, bleak and hard and unforgiving. In *The Four-Gated City* she gave me a sense of a London that I had never met before, not harsh on a grand scale as Dickens's or Defoe's London was, or frivolous and class-bound in the fashion of Fielding and Thackeray, but mean and low and second-rate on the inevitable morning after a great cataclysm, a formerly dominant nation that now felt itself slipping into a stature more commensurate with its physical size. Early in the book Martha Quest walks through the Thameside neighborhood hit hard by the war:

About three acres lay flat, bared of
building. Almost—it was a half job;
the place had neither been cleared, nor
left. It was as if some great thumb had
come down and rubbed out buildings,
carelessly: and then the owner of the
thumb had blown away bits of debris
and rubble, but carelessly. All the loose
rubble had gone, or been piled up
against walls, or the fence; but pits of
water marked old basements, and sharp
bits of walls jutted, and a heap of gird-
ers rusted.

From this landscape, surely, and the subsequent years
in which the Soviet Union and the United States went
on to be superpowers locked in a cold war and England
to look on as their wise, slightly doddery uncle, arose
that assurance my friend once gave to me that the great
days of the U.K. were over and position and privilege
now lay inevitably across the Atlantic.

The British people, especially those younger members who were born after the bombs had fallen, even
after the vacant lots were cleared and rebuilt, surely
must tire of hearing about the indomitability of their
fathers and mothers in the face of that devastation. But

Doris Lessing in 1981

its sheer indomitability is one of the great appeals of London in a sky-is-falling culture. "Business as usual," Churchill said during the war, and business as usual might be the British motto, even today.

Certainly there is none of this air of rediscovering the wheel of history that prevails among Americans. At the height of the controversy about invading Iraq and the animosity that ensued between the United States and England and the French, a limo driver waxed poetic and specific about 1,200 years of French perfidy. Then he concluded with a nod, "But it all sorted itself out. We finished with more of their land than they had, didn't we now?" It was difficult not to think of one of the prettiest pieces in the British Museum show, an enormous brooch of gold, silver, enamel, and rock crystal, the president's badge of the Anti-Gallican Society. The society was founded in 1745 "to oppose the insidious arts of the French nation," and the brooch is engraved with its motto "For our country" and St. George on a white horse running his spear gleefully through a fleur-de-lis. There were Anti-Gallican teacups and china, too. "It goes back a long way," said the driver with a nod.

And yet the English have learned to adapt, if not to forgive and forget. Just opposite Fortnum and Mason, the enormous food emporium so beloved of Anglophiles, there is now a Japanese confectionery with sweets made of rice and bean paste, as beautiful as flowers nestled in their tiny wicker baskets. The notice board for the changing of the guard at Buckingham Palace is in French as well as English, but also in German and in Japanese, despite the damage to the selfsame palace inflicted during the war.

Little of central London betrays any signs of that damage. Only the eldest residents can see retrospectively, the street as it appears today and as it once was, before the bombs. Rebirth is the theme instead. The scaffolds that mask the elegant facades from Notting

Hill to St. James's Palace speak of an era of indulgent rebuilding, not the reconstruction of deprivation and necessity but the adding of noise-resistant windows, new baths and kitchens. Strolling through those neighborhoods with our guidebooks, we tend to be a bit contemptuous of the new high-rise with no more character or ornament than a canvas awning to the street provides. We can forgive American cities their banal architecture (except, perhaps, for Houston); but not London. Not with all the beauty that surrounds us.

But what the guidebooks cannot tell is how the newer buildings rose there. In New York we know that, in almost every case, some benighted group or individual decided to trade in, say, the glorious neoclassic Penn Station for a hideous modern thing that appears to be the bastard child of a factory and a public school auditorium. But in London much of the modern rises on the bones of the antique because the antique was blown away in the Blitz. It is one of those moments when what has vanished teaches more than what remains.

CHAPTER TWELVE

Perhaps it was only the offerings in our school
library, but there seemed to me as a girl to be a
disproportionate number of stories, skewed specifically
to the preteen set, about Elizabeth I. This was fine
with me. At a threshold level the appeal was obvious:
a pampered child, an adolescent outcast, an accident of
birth, an accident of death, and then, greatness. It had
all the elements of a great novel with a young girl at
its center, and the happiest of endings for some of us
who were beginning to feel the talons of worldly am-
bitions clawing at our midsections, later summed up
in the pop feminist slogan: I am my own prince.

Although, in Elizabeth's case, it might more properly have been: I am my own queen. And that of most of the known world.

But like so many of the most compelling English novels, the story of Elizabeth threw out tendrils that led to other engrossing tales. As Trollope's novels of Parliamentarian intrigue led one to the other, with characters entering and departing the dance and some, like Plantagenet Palliser and his wife, the spirited Lady Glencora, appearing as perennials, growing older, wiser, or perhaps only cannier, so Elizabeth's story led backward and forward to others. The young Henry, loving his brother's widow, then casting her off for someone younger and wilder. The younger, wilder Anne Boleyn, holding the King at arm's length, then succumbing, finally disappearing into the Tower, telling the executioner, according to legend, that he needn't worry, that she had a little neck. And Elizabeth's siblings, the unhappy and pious Lady Mary and the sickly and short-lived Edward. Later there would be the fops and intrigues of the Restoration, and the offspring of Victoria, populating the palaces of the world. These were sagas, too, but none of them could hold a candle to that of the Tudors and the redheaded goddess at the center of their story.

And that was despite the fact that, for young people's consumption, these histories of the time glossed over the more provocative, uglier facts. None of the stories of the young Elizabeth checked out from my Catholic school library were explicit about her parent's marriage, driven by lust, or their schism, in which Anne was accused of having sex with, among others, her own brother. None told of how Elizabeth's last stepmother married a nobleman who may have molested the girl, or of how she dangled her virginity in front of every reigning monarch in Europe to keep the region in a state of dizzy disequilibrium. In all those books Elizabeth was described as she liked to describe herself, the Virgin Queen, but to a child raised on the Virgin Mary, this seemed to have less to do with sex and more with importance and position.

Yet all the stories seemed to have one plot twist in common, and that was that London was the prize. When Catherine of Aragon, past her childbearing years, was discarded by her now-aged boy king, she was sent from the city. When Elizabeth was displaced by the disgrace of her mother and the birth of her brother, she was sent away as well, out to the English countryside. In rural beauty, becalmed, she awaited the summons back. To be restored to London was to be restored to the place where her mother Anne had reached the zenith of her short career: arrived at the Tower while the Thames teamed with gaudily decorated boats, rode through the streets in a litter of cloth of gold dressed in ermine and jewels, was crowned in Westminster Abbey while all the lords and ladies of the court looked on. To return to London was to return to life—a life of color, confusion, intrigue, crosscurrents, but a life fully lived.

Of course, not everyone felt that way, then and now. English literature, and English life, are filled with those who are overwhelmed, exhausted, and repelled by life in the cheek-by-jowl metropolis, not the least of them reigning monarchs. Prince Charles is said to be more at home in his gardens at Highgrove, his country estate, than he is in the palatial quarters he occupies in central London. His mother the Queen looks most herself in photographs when she is pictured in the country, a scarf tied over her hair, Wellington boots on her feet, and a pack of dogs eddying around her. In fact, many of the pleasures of English life we foreigners have learned about through books tend to be country pleasures: dogs, horses, especially gardening.

This is clear in many of the most beloved English novels. Agatha Christie would much prefer to be in St. Mary Mead with Miss Marple or even on a cruise with Hercule Poirot then set down in the center of Chelsea. Austen is famously unequivocal in *Emma* when the hypochondriacal Mr. Woodhouse says stoutly, "The truth is, that in London it is always sickly season. Nobody is healthy in London, nobody can be." (This sentiment stands in opposition to the oft-quoted—too oft-quoted, actually—sentiment of Samuel Johnson that "when a man is tired of London, he is tired of life.")

In her memoirs Jessica Mitford recalled her father's trips: "On very rare occasions he lumbered into his London clothes and with much heavy breathing prepared for the trip—always considered a tremendously arduous journey, although it was actually only eighty miles—to sit in the House of Lords." By contrast to the exile of the Elizabethans, in any number of English novels the good folks of the shires travel to the capital, or "to town," as it is so often described, only under duress, and when they return to the villages and estates which they consider their proper homes a reader can almost feel them take in a lungful of good clean air.

Initially, of course, this was for simple sanitary reasons. The streets of long ago London were punctuated by enormous garbage piles; one afternoon, as I watched a man with a begrimed face pick through a trash basket in Regent's Park, I realized that I'd met his like before, in Dickens and in the diaries of Samuel Pepys, in the person of the trash pickers and vendors who made their living off the refuse.

But the garbage was not the worst of it. Even a sheltered young reader could, sooner or later, figure out what was inside a "slops jar" and what would be the net effect of throwing its contents out an upstairs window in what, half a millennium ago, was the most populous city in Europe. Disease ran rampant in London because sewage did. London Bridge had a public toilet, the contents of which went directly into the Thames. It is one thing to stand in the grand semicircle of Trafalgar Square and admire how the terrain slopes gently down to Big Ben and from there to the river, quite another to consider how important that was during the era when raw sewage ran through the gutters directly into the water. Even when the gutters were replaced by sewers, the sewers fed right into the famous river, until the water was brown, the water birds died, and members of Parliament talked of leaving Westminster because of the fumes. The Big Stink, it was called before it was remedied in the nineteenth century.

But it was not just the noisome air that drove the determination, evident in so many English novels, to stay safely away from London. There was the stench of evil, too, or at least license, so at odds with the sense of village rectitude. The eighteenth century, for instance, marked the heyday of what, in Heyer's romance novels, is known as the "ton," a class of cynical dandies who stood prevailing standards of good behavior on their head. Husbands and wives were expected to spend little time together; infidelity was de rigueur. (Hence this tight-lipped exchange in a Heyer novel, *Devil's Cub,* one of her typical tales of true love amid the debauchery: "He frowned. 'Orgies, Fanny?' 'Orgies, Hugh. Pray do not ask more.'")

Stories reached the landed gentry of the escapades of Georgiana, Duchess of Devonshire, the queen of ton society, who used padding to make her upswept hair three feet high, who performed onstage and gambled her husband's money away, who spoke in a peculiar form of baby talk called the Cavendish Drawl. When Sheridan wrote *The School for Scandal,* Georgina was the model for the lead role of the good-hearted but loose-living Lady Teazle. But while the upright people of Devon or Kent would have been outraged to see themselves so portrayed, Georgiana's circle went to the theater to be seen watching a farce, as good as watching themselves and their own dissolute customs.

A century later Victoria had set a more rigid standard, but there were still stories that made London seem like a different, less ordered world than the villages and towns. Victoria's eldest son, the pleasure-loving Prince of Wales, had a deer brought to the center of the city, perhaps in an attempt to re-create the hunting parties of

Henry VIII that led to the creation of London's most beautiful parks. With his pals, the Prince chased the animal through Harrow and Wormwood Scrubs, cornering and killing it at Paddington Station while railway porters goggled at the sight. The newspapers editorialized darkly about the royal misbehavior.

Even the novelists passed judgment harshly. Reading Trollope's two great series of novels, one set largely in town, the other in the country, it is manifest that the folks of the Barsetshire chronicles are less hard, cold, and calculating than those we meet in London in the company of the Pallisers. Like the Mitford father, the aged country gentry eschew the city unless absolutely necessary. Sir Alured Wharton may be a baronet, but one "not pretending to the luxury of a season in London for which his modest three or four thousand a year did not suffice." Trollope adds, "Once a year he came up to London for a week, to see his lawyers, and get measured for a coat, and go to the dentist." Why venture into the city more? In *The Prime Minister*, every fashionable street is populated by those whose very names are meant to suggest their venality and dissolution: Sir Damask and Lady Monogram, Mr. Hartlepod, Lord Mongrober, the Marquis of Mount Fidgett. ("Now the late Marquis had been, as was the custom with the Fichy Fidgett, a man of pleasure. If the truth may be spoken openly, it should be admitted that he had been a man of sin.") These are manifestly not nice people, and, predictably, when his daughter is enmeshed in an unacceptable love affair, the upright Mr. Wharton's first thought is that he "must take her away from London." A reader knows at the finale of the novel that Emily Wharton is finally safe because she will spend the rest of her life with the good folks of Herefordshire, of whom her first husband, sophisticated and dishonest, had been so dismissive.

In modern day London there is little talk of the evil that once inspired country folks to stay put and city folks to leave. All the evils of the metropolis—drugs, prostitution, pornography—are now available almost anywhere on Earth, even in sleepier shires. Some of those who prefer the country life speak of London's grime and crime, although even a cursory look back through the history of the capital shows that in the past it has been far dirtier and far less safe. (In one of the most dramatic scenes in *The Prime Minister,* two young men of fashion go for a drunken late night walk through St. James's Park, although they know it is foolhardy; sure enough, they are promptly mugged. In every regard the story seems completely contemporary.)

But the current fashionable reasons for leaving London are more pedestrian in a somewhat depressing fashion. The *Sunday Times* featured the issue one day in its real estate supplement and focused on the families of the Wandsworth section of the city, who find it less "child-friendly" than the greener regions and are moving out of town in droves. "The thought of trying to get on the Tube with a buggy horrifies me," one young mum complained. A far cry from the stench of evil that the shires once believed emanated from the city.

CHAPTER THIRTEEN

Not so long ago there was a billboard at the Hogarth roundabout on the way to the airport that had some parents in the area in a swivet. It read "Roger More" and was an advertisement for a brand of condoms. Most Americans probably thought it was a misprint and that someone had inexplicably left out the second *o* in the last name of the British actor who once played James Bond.

That's because the term "roger" is nothing but a name in the United States, while in England it's a slang expression for having sex. Condoms, however, are not also known as rubbers, as they are in America. Rubbers are the things we call erasers.

I actually know a good bit of this. I have long taken a great satisfaction in the fact that I speak English. Real English, not the tongue Americans speak. I have virtually no facility with languages—my schoolgirl French just barely enables me to get laundry sent out or a sweater purchased and paid for in Paris. But as a young reader, little by little I began to assemble a vocabulary that bore no relationship to that used by the average American child. I am proud to say that I scarcely ever used it in conversation, although occasionally I would try to use Englishisms in my writing, and my teachers would underline an exclamation like "Bollocks!" or the description of someone as "daft" and write in the margin, "What are you trying to say here?" (One old nun, I remember, once wrote, "You can read Dickens without trying to be Dickens." As if being Dickens was even possible!)

It was a useful bit of self-education, because all of my translation had to be done from context. What precisely were elevenses, and how did they differ from tea? How was tea different from high tea, if at all? What were O levels, and how did one attain a first at Oxford or Cambridge? If fags were cigarettes and pissed was drunk, what did vulgar Brits call it when they had to urinate or wanted to mock homosexuals? A nice piece of fish—plaice, usually, which seemed to be flounder—

was lovely. A day in the country was brilliant. Bonk meant having sex, too, and knickers were underpants; before I tumbled to this, I was constantly perplexed by the state in which various English heroines found themselves in the bedroom, as though they were ready to play golf before bed.

Americans don't use Englishisms much, although, from time to time, you do pass an American bar actually named "Ye Olde English Pub." This extends to other products and services; recently an American catalog company featured a Portobello coat, Carnaby boots, and a Savile tee shirt, the last particularly puzzling given the legendary tailoring of Savile Row suits. What could a Savile tee shirt possibly look like? Lapels? Handsewn seams and darts?

Of course, the problem with appropriating the English language from books rather than overheard life was that much of it was antiquated. Or, perhaps in some cases, invented. When Waugh describes how his madcap partygoers "all got into two taxicabs and drove across Berkeley Square—which looked less than Arlenish in the rain," is he using a common piece of slang, one that came and went with the Charleston, or one he simply invented? In Georgette Heyer's popular Regency novels, there is a really lovely piece of slang: People are always warning their friends "not to make a cake out of yourself," which obviously means not to behave foolishly. But it's a piece of slang that is apparently as dead and buried as George III; no contemporary English man or woman I've asked had ever heard it, except for one pleasant professor who had a passing familiarity with antiquated language. (On the other hand, "he's a bit wet," English for "he's kind of a geek," is alive and well and as alluring a turn of phrase as I've ever encountered in real life.)

During all those years of reading *A Christmas Carol*, we were never entirely sure what was meant when Fezziwig, in the midst of a dance in which he and his wife were "top couple," was said with great admiration to have "cut." In fact the word itself is in quotations, as though even in Dickens's time it was too slangy to stand alone. Since the description continues, "cut so deftly, that he appeared to wink with his legs," the five of us have decided that what Fezziwig does is what we call a split.

But until recently we had no idea why the boy Scrooge asks to buy the prize turkey for the Cratchit family after his spiritual resurrection replies, "Walk-ER!" Even on my English trips, I got no more than a puzzled look. ("That sounds very much like one of those cockney phrases Americans insert in films," one English editor said dryly.) My son and I were therefore enormously chuffed to discover in the Ackroyd book that the word was a piece of street slang that "lasted three or four months only" at the beginning of the nineteenth century, and therefore was probably a remnant of Dickens's boyhood. "It was used by young women to deter an admirer, by young boys mocking a drunk, or to anyone impeding the way," Ackroyd writes. Mystery solved. (And another wonderful turn of phrase added: "What a shocking bad hat!" contemporaneous with Walk-ER and aimed at anyone of really singular appearance.)

Not only is this no longer the language of London, but English is in some ways no longer the language of London. One study showed that more than three hundred languages are now spoken in the city's schools, from Bengali, Punjabi, and Urdu to Cantonese and Jamaican patois. ("Babelians," Zadie Smith calls them in her novel of the new immigrant London, *White Teeth.*) And American slang and usage has become such a consistent presence, not only because of visitors but because of exported rap music and sitcoms, that the lines between argots are relatively porous. While once we were warned to ask for the bill, not the check, and to order a sweet, not dessert, almost no wait staff in a London restaurant looks twice if you ask the American way.

This does not work both ways, however; one English visitor told of the general hilarity that ensued when she ordered pasta in a New York restaurant, pasta being pronounced in England in a way that more or less rhymes with "master." Nevertheless, there are certainly times when the English treat their American cousins like subverbal idiots; perhaps the concierge did not realize he was leaning slightly forward and raising his voice appreciably when he told me about the theater tickets he'd acquired for us: "They are located in the stalls. Stalls. What you call the or-che-stra." It was all I could do not to reply, "I know what the stalls are. I've read Trollope and Ngaio Marsh!"

On the other hand, the poor man had probably had his own language trials, judging by the performance one night in Piccadilly Circus by a group of drunken American men in Union Jack tee shirts who were having what they considered an uproarious conversation that seemed to consist entirely of the expressions "cheerio" and "bloody." Of course, one of them also felt moved to quote from *Wayne's World* about Piccadilly Circus: "What a shitty circus! Where're all the tigers and clowns?"

The other problem with learning language from books is that literature frequently reflects an exaggerated form of normal dialogue. Huck Finn and Holden Caulfield, for instance, have a hyperannuated adolescent voice that bears homage to, but doesn't always mirror exactly, the footloose orphan of the nineteenth century or the disenchanted prep school boy of the twentieth. Surely the Pickwickians speak like a series of playlets—not surprising given Dickens's affinity for the theater—not like actual human beings.

In fact, while I had managed to wend my way through various novels, had come to understand what it meant when Rumpole's father-in-law referred to the Old Bailey as "not exactly the SW1 of the legal profession," I was not really prepared to use these locutions in real life. And I was certain I had no idea how to pronounce many of the words I had learned to recognize with my eyes: How in the world did you actually say Cholmondeley or Gloucestershire? It remains a source of shame to me that through much of my girlhood I pronounced the name of the river that runs famously through London with the "th" fully articulated and a long *a* after. "Thames," one of my high-school teachers finally said, "rhymes with gems." As a reader, English place-names had become what Russian surnames had always been: something to register with the mind and the eye but never to venture with the tongue.

These concerns, too, were put off because I never actually visited London, until I hired as a nanny for our firstborn (the very selfsame writer mentioned above) a Mancunian woman, late the manager of a rock-and-roll band. (Until I met Kay, I would have thought a Mancunian was a person who came from some exotic foreign land, not someone who came from Manchester.) Early on we got into a frustrating rondelay about whether my son had any vests or jumpers. Eventually it became clear that Kay was referring to what I knew as undershirts and sweaters, and I showed her where they had been packed away after the baby shower. Over time sometimes I called them vests, and sometimes she called them undershirts. (Once there was a contretemps over a "dummy," which turned out to be a term that had never crossed my field of vision during my reading. This was a pacifier. I don't believe in them.) Eventually we even developed some conversational Englishisms around the house; for example, when one evening my husband felt moved to tell Kay that he found completely unintelligible her Mancunian accent—which, in his defense, even some Londoners find challenging—she replied, "Sod off, Gerry." This became a term of art around the house for months to come, despite the fact that my *Lonely Planet British Phrasebook* informs me that its origins are in the word "sodomy." But the explanation continues, "Most British people who use this term don't mean anything sexually menacing by it ... you may consider yourself insulted, but not too much."

The fact that there exists a British phrasebook to, in its words, "avoid embarrassing British–U.S. differences" says a great deal about the language chasm between the two. It's been often remarked upon, and sometimes it goes both ways, although most of the time the Americans are the philistines. The Irish writer John Connolly, for example, has decided for whatever reason to set his suspense novels in various parts of the United States. (It's probably the same impulse that has led Californian Elizabeth George to write a series of books about a titled inspector for Scotland Yard.) But Connolly blew it in a small way in a recent novel when his American hero put on a pair of trainers, a term of art for sneakers that few people in Maine or Louisiana would ever have heard of. On the other hand, one editor at a British publishing house was trying to see that one of her American writers made it across the pond successfully and wasn't sure there wasn't a glitch in a manuscript she'd gotten. "How would you describe chicken-fried steak?" she asked. (Yuck.)

You can tell a really wonderful quote by the fact that it's attributed to a whole raft of wits. Such is the quip about America and England being two countries divided by a common language. Churchill, I was told definitively by one student of modern history. Shaw, said an inveterate reader. But a quotations dictionary has it as Oscar Wilde ("We have really everything in common

Oscar Wilde during his tour of the United States and Canada in 1882

with America nowadays, except, of course, language.")
and another Bertrand Russell ("It is a misfortune for
Anglo-American friendship that the two countries are
supposed to have a common language.") I feel quite
chuffed about being able to speak English English
until I actually do it. Then I find myself in Southwark,
pronouncing (or mispronouncing) the *w,* and find
myself thinking of Wilde. Or Russell. Or Churchill.
Or whomever it may have been.

CHAPTER FOURTEEN

The idea of a Literary London alongside the literal city is not a new one. There are courses on the subject for everyone from tourist groups to university students and even a scholarly journal with papers on such subjects as "Theatrical Spectacles and the Spectators' Positions in Wordsworth's London." The English are not above playing the literary card; at one hotel in Mayfair, the apartment suites are named after great writers, the Fielding, the Austen. In the window of Rule's, purportedly London's oldest restaurant, the stuffed pheasants in the window vie for attention with information about past diners, Dickens and Thackeray among them. And why not? If America confers luster on a home by saying "Washington slept here," how can anyone be expected to resist the temptation to say "Shakespeare wrote here." Not only wrote, but wrote triumphantly of his surroundings:

> *This royal throne of Kings, this scept'red isle,*
> *This earth of majesty, this seat of Mars,*
> *This other Eden, demi-paradise,*
> *This fortress built by Nature for herself*
> *Against infection and the hand of war,*
> *This happy breed of men, this little world,*
> *This precious stone set in the silver sea,*
> *Which serves it in the office of a wall,*
> *Or as a moat defensive to a house,*
> *Against the envy of less happier lands,*
> *This blessed plot, this earth, this realm,*
> *this England.*

No country needs more than that. And yet there is so much more in the syllabus for the Literary London courses and tours that abound. There's Chaucer and a trip to the Guildhall, Shakespeare and the roughhewn replica of the Globe on the South Bank of the Thames, Poet's Corner and Chelsea, and, of course, the Dickens House. The books and places most of the courses use and cite don't change much. Fashions in literature do, of course. Galsworthy out, Bowen out and then in again, Woolf in only for modernists of a certain stripe until, that is, the movies took her up. My old clothbound *History of English Literature,* circa 1885, declares: "There are two distinguished authors, who divide the honour of being called 'First novelist of the day.' Charles Dickens and William Makepeace Thackeray stand side by side on that proud eminence, each with his multitude of admirers." But the on-line reading list for Kingston University today states flatly, "The great figure of nineteenth-century literary London is Charles Dickens." Poor Thackeray.

Each of the reading lists for these Literary London surveys tends to end with the same modern writers. But those "modern" writers are often those who wrote seventy or eighty years ago, Woolf, Bowen, along with slightly more contemporary names: Julian Barnes, Hanif Kureishi, Jeanette Winterson. Much is made of Martin Amis's novel *London Fields.*

But *London Fields* is not a novel that is particularly evocative of London in any way, nor are most of its counterparts. The literary novels of London have become less about place and more about psychology, less about class per se and more about ethnicity. And modern London, like most other great capitals, has become more like everywhere else in a way that makes specificity in writing about it both less possible and less useful.

It may seem a frivolous example, but I'm frequently struck by how all of this plays out in shopping. When I was a child and my parents traveled to Europe, they returned with presents that were specific and exotic, the sorts of things that were not readily available in the United States. From Spain, a heavily embroidered shawl. From Rome, beautiful leather boots. From Copenhagen, clogs—"what *are* those?" my friends would ask. From Ireland, fisherman's sweaters. From London, tweed jackets. These were the marks of having traveled.

But, of course, now we can buy Italian shoes and English woolens nearly anywhere in the world, just as nearly anyone in the world can buy those great American exports, the Quarter Pounder with Cheese and the Gap jean. New Bond Street in London is, as it has been in countless books and histories, a wonderful place to shop, but it is no more English than I am. Chanel, Tiffany, Donna Karan, Cartier: The English luxe purveyors are outnumbered by foreign competitors and, sadly, the same foreign competitors whose stores can be found in Paris and Toronto, Hong Kong and Las Vegas, surely in New York. Conversely, there is now a Burberry store in many American cities, and Harris tweeds can be found everywhere. Even William Evans offers a Web site for hunting gear and jackets, plus fours straight from the London store via FedEx.

There were those halcyon days during the 1960s and, later, in a smaller way, at the end of the century, when London had a hip cachet unheard of elsewhere in the world. The Beatles, Mary Quant, the Sex Pistols, the punk movement: The city had once again become the world capital, this time of cool. Cool Britannia: That was the catch phrase that all the magazines used as they turned London, a city for the ages, into flavor of the month.

But cool is a commodity that runs wild as soon as it is let loose and never, ever, acknowledges its roots, and before you could say Led Zeppelin or Haight-Ashbury, America had buried its former forefather. Not long ago I was cabbing it to Notting Hill, the new cool London neighborhood (even as I write this I know, in the nature of things, that some other place has likely supplanted it), when the cab driver slowed appreciably. "That is the home of Madonna," he said solemnly. Who is, of course, the Quarter Pounder with Cheese of celebrities, American, middlebrow, famous worldwide.

Even the men who sell souvenirs along the iron gates of St. James's Park are selling the same souvenirs, with slight adaptations, that their compatriots are selling opposite the Metropolitan Museum of Art on Fifth Avenue thousands of miles away. Florid oil paintings of a barely recognizable generic city. Sweatshirts with the Union Jack instead of the American flag. Even the ubiquitous tee shirt, now gone worldwide: "My grandparents went to (fill in the blank) and all I got was this lousy tee shirt."

Shouldn't it at least read "bloody tee shirt?"

The net effect is to make everywhere feel somehow the same, and nowhere feel particularly particular. What a metaphor it seems to compare and contrast the most splendid and the most recent portraits of the monarch in the Queen's Gallery at Buckingham Palace. The glory of the place is a portrait by van Dyck of Charles I riding on a handsome, romantically rendered horse: enormous, overwhelming, larger than life-size in a baroque gilt frame. Its twin, I suppose, is the portrait of Elizabeth II presented by the artist Lucian Freud in 2001. It is about the size of a sheet of writing paper, and shows the Queen wearing the astonishing diamond diadem, on display elsewhere in the gallery, atop her familiar lacquered bouffant.

Yet, despite the crown, the Queen looks like a peevish aging housewife. There is nothing of splendor in the image: This is a quite ordinary woman incongruously bejeweled. One can only conclude that if Freud had painted such an image—realistic, no doubt—of Charles I, he would have been summarily executed. Ditto for the architects of the Millennium footbridge, opened to much fanfare—and months late—to celebrate twenty-first-century London. Reporters trooped across it en masse, and as they did it began to undulate up and down, side to side, until eventually members of the press were clinging to its sides. (Those familiar with the English press speculated that this was not, in fact, a mistake.) The engineering problems have since been resolved, and the new bridge joins the other legendary spans across the Thames. But there's no doubt that if such a bridge had been built by Henry VIII for some grand occasion and had rattled about in such a fashion on its maiden voyage, heads would have rolled.

It would certainly be simple to decry this, to do as older Londoners do and sigh and frown and complain that the old place just isn't as it was, as it was before the war, after the war, before the boom, before the bust, before the arrivistes and the new rich. But why ought the novels of today's London mimic their forebears? Where's the creativity (for writers) and the amusement (for readers) in that? The question seemed to be answered visually in the courtyard of Burlington House, which stands back from the throng of Piccadilly like an outraged dowager lifting her satin skirts. The Earl of Burlington's town mansion is now the home of the Royal Academy, and, before its famous summer exhibition got underway in 2003, workmen were busy erecting a statue in the courtyard. The figure appeared to parallel the monument to Sir Joshua Reynolds, the eighteenth-century neoclassicist president of the Royal Academy; the sculpture stood catty-corner from Reynolds, facing him, triumphant on a pedestal, a torch in his hand. But, on closer examination, the torch was a microphone, the figure wearing jeans, and his physique not that of Greek statuary but of the modern health club and weight machines. (No Athenian was ever so ripped!) And inside the pedestal was a propane tank, so that from time to time the mike would spew a plume of fire. Perhaps the statue was an ironic comment on the bewigged figure facing it, cast in bronze, holding an artist's palette. But it appeared to be imitation without reason.

The literature of London now reflects its modernity, as it should. It also reflects, less happily, the everywhere-is-anywhere ethos of easy air travel and effortless chain imports that has homogenized most of the developed world. Only the detective novels, perhaps needing some firm undeniable bedrock for their uncommon tales of murder, blackmail, and back channel plots, still draw heavily upon clear and specific delineations of place. And even one of the detectives of P. D. James—Baroness James, now, as London continues to pay homage to literature—lives in the new London, in

P. D. James in 1987

a modern flat facing "the huge shining pencil" of
Canary Wharf and the contemporary sprawl of
Docklands.

Yet this change in arts and letters is all part of a discernible continuum, too. The descriptions of London in
the novels of Martin Amis, for example, are as perfunc-
tory as those in Defoe, but for quite different reasons.
While Moll Flanders rattles off the names of the streets
she travels with little or no description because her

creator could be confident that his readers would be able to effortlessly conjure up the location, Amis's protagonists do so because detailed descriptions of place are not the point in his novels, in which human psychology is both theme and location. "Chelsea, Blackfriars, Regent's Park, Bloomsbury, Hampstead, and so on," he says of one nomadic character. But for the extent to which these places are important in the action of the book, he could just as well have written "Chelsea, Tribeca, Park Slope, Greenpoint, and so on," substituting the names of New York neighborhoods. The novel owes very little to a sense of specific place, and Amis seems to have considered the city in which he lives as little more than a platform for the universal anomie of his characters. It is only at the very end of *London Fields* that he becomes a flagrant Londoner, when he adds, in a kind of coda, "The people in here, they're like London, they're like the streets of London, a long way from any shape I've tried to equip them with, strictly non-symmetrical, exactly lopsided."

Ethnicity, too, has become its own setting, so that novels of the immigrant experience are among some of the best and most successful that modern London can offer. But again, they are rarely portraits of a place. The family of Monica Ali's *Brick Lane* is so claustrophobically contained within the housing project and the ethnic enclave in which they live that it is a shock to the reader when, more than halfway through the novel—and more than thirty years after the head of the household has arrived in London—they visit Buckingham Palace. An American tourist, his accent "familiar from television," asks where they are from and the husband's reply is, "We are from Bangladesh." His wife is as dismissive of Buckingham Palace as Virginia Woolf had been in *Mrs. Dalloway* decades before: "If she were Queen she would tear it down and build a new house, not this flat-roofed block but something elegant and spirited, with minarets and spires, domes and mosaics, a beautiful garden instead of this bare forecourt. Something like the Taj Mahal."

Between these modern writers who trade street atmospherics for the interior world of the psyche and the early English novelists who assumed a reader's knowledge of their locale and so little thought to limn it come centuries of others whose work falls between the two poles. There are the years of Dickens and Thackeray, with their rich and ornamented descriptions of the city, a function of the style of the times and, perhaps, the presumed eye of foreign readers. There are the elegiac descriptions as the glorious empire gave way to one small island, the satire of Waugh and the despair of Forster, a sense of a certain sort of dominant and

Brick Lane, center of London's Bangladeshi community

indomitable London slowly slipping away. "Today
Whitehall had been transformed," writes Forster, who
clearly loved the place and feared for it, too. "It would
be the turn of Regent Street tomorrow. And month by
month the roads smelt more strongly of petrol, and were
more difficult to cross, and human beings heard each
other speak with greater difficulty, breathed less of the
air and saw less of the sky."

The passage speaks poetically of the end of something. Yet it is the glory of London that it is always end-
ing and beginning anew, and that a visitor, with a good

eye and indefatigable feet, will find in her travels all the Londons she has ever met in the pages of books, one atop the other, like the strata of the Earth. On the South Bank of the Thames, where the pilgrims of *The Canterbury Tales* began their journey, there now stands silhouetted against the often lowering clouds the newest London landmark, the London Eye, the world's tallest—and certainly most technologically sophisticated—Ferris wheel. It was derided as a bit of a gimmick when it was first proposed, and the plan was to take it down after a few years. But it has become an icon of the city—another icon of a city that perhaps has more iconographic places, buildings, and locations than any other.

Atop it, in one of the glass cars in which tourists ride, it is possible to see most of London. The London that was rebuilt after the enemy bombs wrecked it. The London that was rebuilt after plague and fire ripped through. The London of Holmes and Watson and Nancy and Fagin, of bright young things and enemy bombs. London upon London upon London, a city in which the destruction of the Blitz managed to unearth a section of the original Roman walls nearly two millennia after their construction. No novelist would use such a metaphor; reality is often more heavy-handed than we can afford to be.

It is a grand panorama, the view from this great engineering marvel, this new colossus. But it is no better than the view of the city from St. Paul's enormous gold dome, an icon that has stood the test of an additional three centuries of time. The only difference is that to get to the dome you must take the steps. We are accustomed now to being carried.

Both are marvelous, but neither constitutes my most beloved place in this best beloved of cities. For that you must come down to Earth and wander aimlessly. Maybe just off Sloane Square, or in Cheval Place, or on Burnsall Street, or Elgin Crescent. Maybe in Notting Hill or South Kensington or Bloomsbury. Finally you will reach it: a house with a bay window or a fanlight over a door, a house with a handsome gate or a small garden.

Around it, a street or two away, swirls the clamor of one of the busiest cities on Earth. Inside is—what? Did a debutante once wait there for her car? Did a maid slip out to meet her lover? Did street peddlers sell ribbons here, or fruit and flowers? Does it stand on the ruins of an older house, or a cow pasture, or even a Roman fort? Did the bombs shake its foundation and the modern real estate boom triple its value?

Behind every door in London there are stories, behind every one ghosts. The greatest writers in the history of the written word have given them substance, given them life.

And so we readers walk, and dream, and imagine, in the city where imagination found its great home.

ACKNOWLEDGMENTS

B y the time I had finished *Imagined London,* I had built
a large castle around me. It was constructed completely of books. Whenever I left my desk, I would have to
find my way through a passage I'd engineered between
travel guides and literary criticism. In the process I broke
the binding on a perfectly good Fodor's, ruined two paperback editions of Dickens I left out in the rain, and dog-eared
and underlined some of the greatest classics ever written.

I also had the time of my life, some of it spent in a
small hotel in Mayfair sharing a suite—and several end-
less televised cricket matches—with Quindlen Krovatin,
the writer and reader who is also my son.

First and foremost I must thank him for all the work he did on this book, and for the pleasure of his company. I couldn't have been habitually lost in London with anyone more interesting.

I acquired Peter Ackroyd's remarkable history of London only after I had begun work on this book. I ripped through it in two days, despite its massive size, because it is so intelligent and entertaining. It is probably impossible to write about London without owning a copy.

I could not imagine living life without the writers mentioned in these pages. In a world that seems increasingly senseless and graceless, they bring intelligence to bear on the human condition.